BLACK IS THE COLOR
OF MY TV TUBE

BLACK IS THE COLOR OF MY TV TUBE

Gil Noble

A Lyle Stuart Book
Published by Carol Publishing Group

First Carol Publishing Group Edition   1990

Copyright © 1981 by Gil Noble

A Lyle Stuart Book
Published by Carol Publishing Group

Editorial Offices
600 Madison Avenue
New York, NY 10022

Sales & Distribution Offices
120 Enterprise Avenue
Secaucus, NJ 07094

In Canada: Musson Book Company
A division of General Publishing Co. Limited
Don Mills, Ontario

Queries regarding rights and permissions
should be addressed to: Carol Publishing Group,
600 Madison Avenue, New York, NY 10022

Manufactured in the United States of America

10   9   8   7   6   5   4   3   2   1

Carol Publishing Group books are available at special discounts
for bulk purchases, for sales promotions, fund raising, or
educational purposes. Special editions can also be created to
specifications. For details contact: Special Sales Department,
Carol Publishing Group, 120 Enterprise Ave., Secaucus, NJ 07094

Library of Congress Cataloging-in-Publication Data

Noble, Gil.
    Black is the color of my TV tube.

    Includes index.
        1. Noble, Gil.   2. Television personalities--
United States--Biography 3.   Like it is
(Television program) 4.   Afro-Americans in the
performing arts.   I.   Title.
PN1993.4.N6A33   791.45'092'4   [B]   80-25614
ISBN   0-8184-0538-4

To my wife, for her loving
support and strength throughout
our life together . . . and to
my children, who have brought
me so much joy and pride.

AUTHOR'S NOTE

This book is entitled *Black Is the Color of My TV Tube* because I think it best describes the way in which I look at the TV industry and the world through my perspective as a black man.

BLACK IS THE COLOR
OF MY TV TUBE

INTRODUCTION

My presence in television is the direct result of the black struggle. But for the social upheaval of the fifties and sixties in America, I believe that I would not now be working in television as a news correspondent, weekend anchor man, producer, and host of a week-ly one-hour program.

I say this not out of bitterness or resentment, but because I regard it as fact. I have learned that one of the most important traits a human can develop is the ability to face facts and measure things as they really are. One can then understand one's surroundings and one's place in the world and learn to function intelligently and without self-delusion.

This sense of reality also serves as a moral guideline for individual performance. It clarifies objectives and crystallizes what is to be done during a lifetime. I refer not only to making a living, but more importantly, to the kind of principles on which one makes a personal stand in life.

My awareness of why I can work in TV shapes my attitude and directs all my energies toward defeating bigotry, oppression, and racial bias. This doesn't mean I go through life with a scowl on my face, nor am I unable to communicate with others. But in the course of my work I look out for my people first and last. I don't hate white people. On the contrary, some of my best friends . . .

To those who say that Gil Noble holds a job that enables him to make such a stand, I say, garbage! I could have been any sort of media person. I could have chosen to offend no one and stand for nothing or to be the type of black man who relates more to whites than to his own people. Regardless of what one does for a living, one can find a way to further a cause as easily as one can be a middle-of-the-roader or a do-nothing.

This is where I'm coming from. But where *this* came from is another story. It began on February 21, 1965—the day before my birthday and the day Malcolm X was shot.

CHAPTER 1

It was a cold Sunday. I was living with my wife and children at Amsterdam Avenue and 155th Street in a New York City project apartment house. I had stopped in front of the building to talk with several neighbors, when the resident custodian joined us with the news. "They finally got him," he said curtly.

I was anything but an activist in 1965, nor was I a follower of Malcolm's. In fact, I was a bit afraid of him. My concern was simply to try to provide for my family by working in the letter-of-credit department of the Chase Manhattan Bank, in the Wall Street district.

I was also involved in music and played the piano passably. I had formed a trio, and we worked in several clubs around the city.

My love for music had started in my early teens, when a friend invited me to hear a new record. It was "Laura," by the famous pianist Erroll Garner. The flip side was "Somebody Loves Me," and when I heard it, I flipped! It was piano playing such as I'd never heard before. I recognized instantly the style of music I wanted to be playing. I faced a problem at home, however. My mother played the piano and read music exceedingly well, and she wanted me to play what she liked—classical music. Piano lessons

13

were therefore fruitless. But the day I heard Erroll was devastating for me, so much so that once I was on my own, I bought a piano and taught myself to play all the music that had been injected into my system by that record.

It should be easy to see that the Nation of Islam* and its articulate former spokesman, Malcolm X, held a place quite distant from my priorities. If any element of the civil rights movement had reached me, it was the power of Doctor Martin Luther King. I was awed by the man after hearing him speak in a church when he visited Harlem.

Doctor King's philosophy was moral in the true Christian tradition, and I could easily accept it. The Muslims, on the other hand, wore strange clothes and said frightening things. They called whites devils. I was raised to believe that I had to be twice as good as a white person in order to be *as* good. Moreover, the new media instrument of television gave Malcolm X a bogeyman image, whereas Doctor King was portrayed much more positively.

Therefore, my building custodian's announcement caused mixed emotions. I didn't have to ask whom he meant. Malcolm had been getting to me. His impact had been making an impression that I wouldn't discover until much later.

Everyone talked about the assassination. We stood on our corner and watched as convoys of police cars whizzed northward to the Audubon Ballroom, where the bloody killing had taken place. Cars jammed with black men sped toward the same destination. The evening news was hot with the assassination story, and for many days, Malcolm X was the topic of discussion in Harlem. His funeral was held at the Faith Temple on Amsterdam Avenue, only four blocks from our home.

The atmosphere in the city was thick with fear and tension.

*The Nation of Islam is its correct name. The organization is perhaps better known by the name invented by the white-dominated media—Black Muslims.

14

Word was out that Malcolm's followers were going to start full-scale warfare with the Nation of Islam. The night following the assassination, the Nation's 116th Street mosque was burned to the ground. There were picketing and several turbulent rallies on 125th Street.

I was forced to focus on Malcolm as never before. I heard what he had stood for and what he was trying to accomplish. The most affecting revelation was the quickly circulated recording of a speech Malcolm had made, "Message to the Grass Roots."

One night a neighbor in our project whispered furtively that he knew why Malcolm X had been murdered. He invited me to his apartment and gave me the recording. I heard Malcolm's unedited speech, and I was overwhelmed.

His was not the soaring oratory of Doctor King, who quoted the Bible and talked about the hereafter and the promised land. Malcolm spoke in the vernacular that I was familiar with—street talk. He told the cold, brutal facts of black existence in this country. He told me who I am, and I have kept that knowledge with me ever since, even as I read a newscast now or walk down the corridors of ABC wearing a smile.

Malcolm drew the true picture of my history as a black—that I am an African who was kidnapped and shipped in chains to this country. The message eliminated the neat white connections I had been taught to make with the founding fathers of this country and pointed out that I had not arrived here by free choice as they had. The speech not only exposed what I was and what had happened to me, in an ancestral sense, but also showed who was responsible. The explanation reached into the present, showing that current conditions among black people are the result and continuation of that traumatic historic beginning.

If this makes you think I was exceptionally naïve, let it be said that thousands, if not millions, of other black youths and adults suffered under similar ignorance. A sense of self, of *true* self, was

15

missing in us as a race. And why expect otherwise? We hadn't been given any exposure to the truth. Our schools didn't tell the story; we didn't hear it in our churches; the newspapers, radio, and television told us just the opposite.

We also laughed at the TV version of Amos 'n' Andy, at Beulah, at Sid Caesar and Red Skelton. Movies like *Pinky* and *Lost Boundaries* depicted a world in which it was far nobler to be white. Paul Robeson had been made a nonperson by mass media, and Doctor Du Bois never became a national celebrity for his thoughts and writings, compared to the career of Doctor Alfred Kinsey.

When *The Autobiography of Malcolm X* later hit the bookstalls, I devoured it. For the first time, I was exposed to the people who make being black important. I learned about J. A. Rogers, the brilliant black historian, and gobbled up his voluminous writings. Malcolm's autobiography did more than acquaint me with his life—it motivated me to study history. Malcolm made it clear that his power and effectiveness came from knowledge.

During this painful and stimulating period of awakening, I began my career in broadcasting, at radio station WLIB in Harlem. WLIB is widely known today to New York listeners as one of the first radio stations owned by blacks in the area, if not *the* first. At the time I worked there, however, it was owned by whites.

Before I got that job, I had been doing voice-over radio and TV commercials. I had also gone to an announcing school to "clean up" my speech and thus enhance my marketability. I had been told at an audition that I hadn't got one particular job because of certain "traces" in my speech pattern.

While at announcing school, I was befriended by Dwight Weist, an instructor who was also a staff announcer at CBS. He encouraged me and gave me extra time and attention. I eventually heard that CBS was looking for black announcers, and I auditioned. The opportunity existed only because the civil rights movement had forced many institutions to hire blacks.

My audition was a resounding flop; I was all but laughed out of the studio. An executive invited me into his office and asked if I had ever done announcing work before. When I said no, he said that he could tell and that although he thought I showed some ability, it needed to be developed. He suggested that I get a job at a small radio station where I could get experience, so I started an endless round of interviews.

After "striking mud" at radio stations in Long Island, New Jersey, and Manhattan, I decided to approach WLIB. Harry Novik was then the owner and station manager. He explained that there was an opening for an announcer, but only for three months, until the regular staff member returned from military service. If I wanted the job on a temporary basis, he would hire me with the okay of the man in charge of the news department.

Mr. Novik's office featured a speaker on which he monitored WLIB broadcasts. A newscast had been in progress during the interview, and Novik revealed that the announcer would be the man who would approve or disapprove my hiring. The report sounded as if it were being delivered by a white man, so when Novik took me into the tiny newsroom and introduced me to Bill McCreary, I was shocked to meet the stocky black news director.

The gods smiled on me that afternoon, and I auditioned well enough for Bill to agree to give me the job. I was to report for work the next morning, although he said he didn't know how long it would be before he thought I would be ready to go on the air.

I rushed home to tell my wife, Jean, who didn't act at all surprised; she even seemed to have been expecting the good news.

I had to do something about my job with Chase Manhattan, so I told my supervisor that I wanted to be transferred to the night shift so that I could go to school. They agreed to the change, and I

17

was free to work days at WLIB in Harlem as a fledgling announcer and then hustle downtown to the Wall Street area to the bank. I also spent Saturdays at WLIB.

My salary at the radio station started at $80 per week, and I earned $125 at the bank. Despite the added pressure and long hours, I was so grateful to get the chance to work at WLIB that I would probably have taken the job without pay, just for the chance to learn.

Fortunately for my wife and kids, I didn't have to go to that extreme. Jean was very understanding about the opportunity. She agreed that it was an investment in our future. I still felt guilty about leaving her alone so long to deal with our three small children, especially with another pregnancy underway. But the job at WLIB was the start of a series of events that surpassed even my wildest dreams. I never expected to eventually be working for the flagship station of one of the three largest television networks on earth. Nor did I know that I would host and produce my own show, complete with a staff and a budget at my disposal. At the inception of my career in the media, I certainly had no idea that the focus of my future would be on the black experience. All this and more was still hidden in the future.

"All you need is one good break," said someone wise in the ways of the world. I got my chance and took it.

Radio station WLIB was in the heart of the Harlem community, at 126th Street and Lenox Avenue. It was a small operation, with offices and studios occupying part of the second floor of a building owned by a black insurance company. WLIB was then owned by a Jewish family and had originally started operations out of the nearby Hotel Theresa, at 125th Street and Seventh Avenue.

A handful of people worked at the station. Harry Novik was assisted by a two-man sales department, two secretaries, a staff of five engineers, and a four-man team that held court in a cubbyhole called the newsroom. A half dozen on-air "personalities" included Billy Taylor, who did a jazz show, Joe Bostic, who did a gospel program, Jack "Pear Shape" Walker, who had a top-forty show, and Tommy Smalls, with a rhythm-and-blues show.

A number of community people also used the studio to tape weekend public-service programs—people like George Schyler, Billy Rowe, Skippy Burgess, Taffy Douglas, Evelyn Cunningham, and others. They taped programs dealing with subjects ranging from social gossip to politics.

WLIB was a very profitable operation—for the owners. By selling air time to a myriad of local businesses (mostly white), the station raked in plenty of money. The studio was in a low rental area and the staff was modestly paid.

The real money came from sponsorship deals with the station management. A steady stream of record-company salesmen drifted in and out of the station daily, carrying in one hand the inevitable stack of the latest 45-rpm "hit" recordings. In the other hand, these salesmen carried cash bribes—"gifts" to ensure that the records they peddled *became* hits.

I can't name names, but no one should be shocked to hear that there was graft. It was peanuts compared to the rivers of cash that flowed in and out of the big-time stations downtown. Radio people in the major stations earned good salaries legitimately, but they also took every payola dollar available. People in the business uptown, however, made far less, and for them, payola was almost a bread-and-butter necessity.

In the midst of this fascinating learning experience, I began to get myself together as a professional and as a man. My boss in the newsroom put me on the air the very first day. Delaying the experience would have caused it to mushroom into an even more terrifying thing, but it was traumatic, nevertheless. The five-minute newscast seemed to last all day. I was too far from the mike. The pounding of my heart reduced my voice to a raspy soprano. I had no pacing. The listening audience was probably stopped cold hearing my horrendous first performance.

When I left the announcing booth, everyone in the newsroom avoided my eyes. I feared that I had just completed my first and last newscast. I learned much later that I hadn't done too badly for the first time, that others had done far worse. Mercifully, Bill McCreary gave me a rather thin smile and told me to sit down in front of my typewriter and prepare for the next newscast.

It worked. The news copy was due in twenty-five minutes, and there was much to do. The pressure distracted me from my embarrassment and forced me to concentrate on the next step. I have used this method of curing nervousness on many occasions since.

WLIB broadcasts the news every thirty minutes. The hourly announcement sometimes ran only two minutes and was merely a reading of the current headlines, with the details coming on the half hour. The major portion of the newscast had to be written by the announcer. The Associated Press wire service spewed out a constant stream of stories from all over the world, and we had a telephone beeper system on which we could do recorded interviews using the telephone. Our staff was constantly sent out into the community to cover events in Harlem that made headlines.

The civil rights movement hit full stride in the early sixties, and Harlem was a nerve center. The National Association for the Advancement of Colored People headquarters was in Manhattan, although far from Harlem. The Congress of Racial Equality was in New York, as were the Urban League, the Black Panthers, and the Nation of Islam, all of which operated and held innumerable news conferences in Harlem.

When the federal government responded to the black outcry with massive antipoverty programs, they were centered in Harlem. Hardly a day passed in which we couldn't leave the station to cover a major news story breaking within a few blocks. News reporters and crews from the big radio and television stations hustled to Harlem. Haryou-Act was headquartered in the nearby Theresa Hotel. Congressman Adam Clayton Powell's Abyssinian Baptist Church was a dozen blocks away. Muslim Mosque Number Seven of the Nation of Islam, opened and developed by Malcolm X, was nine blocks away.

The fabled sidewalk orators of 125th Street, "Porkchop" Davis, Charles Kenyatta, James Lawson, and others could be heard every evening delivering their messages on black nationalism, Africa, racism, and other serious topics.

Around the corner from the radio station was Lewis Michaux' historic National Memorial African Bookstore ("The House of Common Sense and Proper Propaganda"). The store was tiny and crammed with books on the black experience. Michaux was a small, witty man who knew the content and location of every book in his store. He would take measure of his customers and figure just what you wanted—or what you needed. The store was a meeting place where one could overhear stimulating debates on black issues. Historians such as John Henrik Clarke and Joseph Ben Jochannan commonly dropped by, very serious and knowing exactly what they were after. They would grab an armful of books, write out a check, and then, if they had the time, talk.

As these men discussed history, past and current, it helped me to clarify my own self-image. I began to understand what and who I was, and to understand the "revolution" that I found myself a part of. In front of the bookstore, facing Seventh Avenue, was the place for rallies. Kwame Nkruma of Ghana came to Harlem and spoke to the community from this site, as did Fidel Castro, Malcolm X, Adam Clayton Powell, Tom Mboya, Martin Luther King, Dwight D. Eisenhower, John F. Kennedy, and scores of other politicians.

I drank in all this like a sponge. My reading picked up and

21

became purposeful. My thinking matured. The more I read and the longer I thought about what I read, the angrier I became. I was touched by the reality of America's brutality against my people, from slavery to the present conditions, and my anger was fueled. That anger still burns.

WLIB was a small radio station, and most staffers performed a wide variety of duties. As a fledgling newscaster, I was assigned chores beyond sitting in an announcement booth and reading a newscast. I serviced the Associated Press teletype machine, which meant making sure that the machine never ran out of paper. I also kept track of interview tapes.

The newsroom had a portable tape recorder that the reporters carried to do interviews. It was heavy but did the job once you got the hang of it. I often began an interview nervously and later discovered that the recorder wasn't working. It was humiliating to be forced to apologize to the interviewee and start the interview again. I devised a ruse of chastising the machine for not working properly, but in retrospect, I don't think I fooled anyone.

Performing all my duties and more gave me a working knowledge of every phase of a newsroom's operation. The pressure of writing a good newscast and delivering it on the air every twenty-five minutes was also important to my training. Eventually I could read my newscast, grab a tape recorder and run down the block to get an interview, race back, edit the tape, hustle to my typewriter, and write the *next* newscast, including the lead-in to the very interview I had just completed! I would then go on the air, and all this within the twenty-five minute span between newscasts. Sometimes there was time to wolf down a sandwich and a soda and even shoot the breeze with one of the disc jockeys.

I was learning how to use a microphone technically—modulating my voice, pacing my reading of the copy, guarding against popping my p's into the mike, talking across the face of

22

the mike instead of directly into it, and judging the correct distance from the microphone. In the beginning I tried to imitate whatever pro I admired, but I gradually came to realize that it was hopeless, and I accepted my own speech patterns and mannerisms.

At the time, broadcast standards were rigid. The networks rated the Midwestern American speech pattern as "ideal." Walter Cronkite's delivery would be the perfect example of what was considered the standard. If one wanted to work in big-time radio announcing, one must learn to talk like Walter Cronkite.

When I went downtown to audition for a major station job and put forth a Cronkite delivery that outdid the original, I was still given the familiar brushoff—"Thanks very much. You're fine, but we already have a Negro on staff." I said, "The hell with it," and went ahead with my work at WLIB, sounding like Gil Noble.

I stayed at WLIB much longer than the originally planned three months.

Ed Williams, whose job I had temporarily held, returned from the military. Ed has gone on to excellence in the business. I managed to hang on to the job by being a little better than another member of the staff, who was eventually let go. I had become an official member of the WLIB news staff by day and an anonymous clerk in the Chase Manhattan Bank's letter-of-credit department by night.

After I had been at the station for a while, I read the contract they had signed with the union (AFTRA) and found that I should have been started at a salary of eighty-five dollars per week instead of the eighty dollars they offered. I contacted the union representative and was told in so many words that I had been given a golden opportunity and shouldn't jeopardize it by asking questions.

Meanwhile, I was getting closer to WABC-TV, but I didn't know it. I had applied for jobs at several big radio and television

23

stations downtown but with no luck. Everyone in the WLIB newsroom was doing the same.

We would sit in the newsroom and fantasize about earning three-hundred dollars a week, but few of our number worked at that level. Pat Connell, a former disc jockey at Newark's WNJR, known as Pat the Cat, was anchoring the CBS morning newscast. Mal Goode was reporting for ABC-TV news, as well as for the local station WABC. NBC didn't have any blacks at that time, as far as I can recall, and in the mid-sixties, WNEW-TV had none, nor did WPIX-TV or WOR-TV have any. Yet we sat in the cramped WLIB newsroom and dreamed, working to perfect our skills.

Something was percolating under America's surface, however, that would make most of us instantly employable.

CHAPTER 2

Until the mid-sixties, the civil rights movement had been explosive but nonviolent. What began in Montgomery, Alabama, with the Rosa Parks incident had become a nationwide drive. The Southern Christian Leadership Conference, headed by the dynamic young Reverend Doctor Martin Luther King, Jr., had grown in numbers and influence. Sit-ins, wade-ins, marches, prayer vigils, and a host of other challenges to America's version of apartheid had been most effective in the South.

It was a different story in the North. Doctor King was shocked to find far more hatred and resistance to change in large urban centers like Harlem and Chicago. Segregation had built strong institutions within the black communities of the South, but in the northern black areas, fragmentation, disunity, and impotence reigned. Some whites in northern cities who were ready and willing to fly south to join desegregation drives were also ready to take up arms to *resist* any desegregation of their home cities. Doctor King's tactics, which had been so successful in the South, were not alleviating northern black conditions. Failure caused frustration and resentment to fester among urban blacks.

Many blacks blamed Doctor King because they did not realize that the womb of racism had been in the North for some time and that this was where the greatest resistance would be. Many brothers and sisters began calling Doctor King a Tom. There arose a different type of resistance—a militant strain.

Attention and allegiance were turned to the Nation of Islam, which preached separation and independence from whites. The words of Malcolm X advised us that we were morally within our rights to defend ourselves from white brutality, since government agencies were unable to protect us. The Black Panther party was organized, with a wide assortment of prescriptions. Young blacks became restless and antagonistic to police corruption and abuse. Explosions occurred and were called riots. Watts, Detroit, Newark, Harlem, Cleveland—everyone knows the places. These actions scared America in ways not felt since the days of Denmark Vesey and Nat Turner.

President Lyndon Johnson appointed a special commission headed by Otto Kerner, the Governor of Illinois, who later went to jail for criminal activity.

This blue-ribbon panel, composed mostly of whites, spent much time and money compiling a report that could have been written by almost any resident of an American black community. The commission report was lengthy and determined that the principal reason for the riots was white racism.

One section, devoted to the mass media, noted that the black presence in the media was almost nonexistent. Therefore, white Americans would never grapple with their own racism until they could be exposed to the black perspective of the situation.

The recommendation was clear and precise: mass media were to hire blacks and put them in visible and meaningful positions "with all deliberate speed." The mass media had been caught with their zippers down. Red-faced executives scurried about, seeking blacks for on-air and other job categories. What more logical place to find black media persons than the so-called soul stations and newspapers? Within a year, many of us found ourselves working

26

downtown at major radio and TV stations.

Bill McCreary was hired by WNEW, Channel 5 News, where he still works; Ed Williams was hired by WCBS-FM radio; Clarence Rock was hired by WINS, the all-news radio station; Roy Davis of WNJR was hired by WNBC, and I was hired by WABC-TV news.

None of the stations said that we were being hired because of the prescriptions of the Kerner Commission's report. They all maintained, and still do, that they are committed to being equal-opportunity companies. If asked about pressure, they would answer, "What pressure?"

The specific means through which we were hired varied. I had seen a reporter named Jim Van Sickle from WABC-TV at news conferences that we covered for our respective stations. We struck up a friendly relationship and always chatted before and after the business at hand.

One day Jim asked, "Why haven't you tried to work with any of the TV news stations?"

I said that I had applied but wasn't having any luck. He told me that there had been a black reporter in the WABC newsroom who had recently left the station. The next day he introduced me to Ed Silverman, the news director of WABC. I talked with Silverman and discovered that there was indeed a job possibility.

No mention was made of Governor Otto Kerner and the report. Silverman asked me to arrange to take a sick day from WLIB and put in a trial day with a camera crew. He then called me before our arranged trial date and told me that one of his reporters would be away on vacation for a week, and he wanted to know if I could arrange to work a full week for WABC-TV, to give him a real opportunity to appraise my work. I agreed.

The next week, I reported for work at WABC-TV news and received my first assignment—covering a fire in lower Manhattan. It wasn't a major fire, but it was perfect fare for the television news, with the visual excitement of the flames, fire engines, coughing evacuees, and firemen. All went well.

My next assignment came out of a late-afternoon report of a disturbance in the black community of Newark, New Jersey. I was advised by the assignment desk to go home but remain on call, "just in case." Those three words were to ensure my employment at Channel 7; they foreshadowed what was to become one of the most momentous upheavals in the metropolitan tri-state area of New York, New Jersey, Connecticut. By nightfall, an incident involving a black youth and a police officer had detonated an explosion of catastrophic proportions in Newark's Central Ward.

I had obeyed the assignment desk clerk's instructions. I was at home watching the six o'clock news for my fire report, when the phone rang and I was ordered to rendezvous with a camera crew in Newark. I drove to the city across the river, parked by Volkswagen downtown, and there hailed a reluctant white cabbie for the trip into the Central Ward. A group of brothers were standing at the corner where I left the cab, and as soon as I moved clear, they showered the car with bricks and rocks.

My press credentials remained in my pocket as I walked through streets thick with smoke, listening to the eerie wailing of fire-engine sirens. Surrounding the Central Ward was a perimeter of police cars and emergency trucks. Beyond those, groups of whites stood, including my all-white camera crew. It was a strange sensation to pass unmolested through the black community and then be forced to show my press card in order to be permitted among the white group.

There was much more confusion on the white side of the barricade than in the parts of town I had walked. Because no one had been in the black area, speculation and rumors of snipers and an "army" of blacks ran through the crowd.

What had happened in the Central Ward was simple: A police

incident had triggered a reaction from people who were poor and frustrated. Many blacks were busy carrying off goods from burned-out stores owned by whites who had been gouging profits from the community for years. These businesses were, for the most part, exploitative, and everyone was aware of that. Now, they were the victims. It is said in the black community: "What goes around, comes around."

The people behind the barricades didn't understand. I saw a few white reporters, and they were terrified. Dusk was quickly gathering, and Mayor Hugh Addonizio (who would later be jailed for another form of looting) called New Jersey's Governor Hughes and requested National Guard assistance to deal with the looting.

I realized that if there *were* snipers, it would be stupid if a random bullet struck me down while I was on the wrong side of the barricades. Reporters were feverishly interviewing police and city government officials, but no one moved to cross the barriers. I decided to enter the Central Ward alone. After walking several blocks, I found a brother observing the melee and explained that I was a reporter. I wanted to take my white cameraman through the Central Ward and film what was happening. Would he drive us around in his car? At first the brother resisted, but then he agreed.

We worked out a place to meet, and I returned to the barricades to persuade the cameraman to accompany me. The brother picked us up, and I rode in front, with the cameraman hidden from sight in the back seat. When I told him to sit up as we approached something worth filming, he popped up with his camera rolling. We got some very good exclusive footage of the situation.

During the drive there were a few moments, when we had stopped to do some filming, when people spotted a "honky" in the back seat of the car and started closing in on us. I once had to urge the driver to get moving as an angry group formed, and he replied that he couldn't because the light was red! "To hell with the traffic light!" I yelled. "There aren't any cops to give you a ticket anyway! If you don't move, that'll be all she wrote!" We lurched through the intersection and escaped.

We shot film all night long and then drove out of the ward to deliver it to a courier who was on his way to the newsroom in New York. Later that night I did a "live" telephone report from the Central Ward during the Bill Beutel 11:00 P.M. newscast. Three sleepless days and nights later, it was all over.

Gil Noble had "made it." The news director decided to hire me. I wearily returned home to tell my wife the good news and was acutely aware of the countless brothers and sisters who were still encircled within the National Guard barricades. Their uprising had been at least partly responsible for my new employment. I continue to keep that knowledge in mind and try to imagine what they would say about the quality of my work now and whether they would consider that I am doing what I ought to be. To Malcolm and many other leaders who made my job possible, I feel the same debt.

Now I could at last earn enough money to give my wife and family a better standard of living. I had quit my job at the Chase Manhattan Bank a year earlier at the request of my dying mother. She had left me a few thousand dollars that I had been drawing on steadily to supplement my meager salary at WLIB. When my audition week for WABC-TV news began, less than a hundred dollars was left in the account.

I've often regretted that my mother died before I got the position at WABC—she would have been pleased. But at least I was in radio and on my way in a career when she died. She did hear me on the air.

My father, however, died more than twenty-five years ago, and at the time, neither he nor I had any idea what I would make of my life. He was a wonderful man—wise, strong, and proud. I wish he were alive to share himself with me today. We would have had so much to talk about.

On the other hand, where is it written that Gil Noble should have a successful and productive career, a wife and children he is proud of, as well as the survival of his parents? For some years now, I have been very good friends with Malcolm's widow. She once made the remark: "Nothing is promised."

CHAPTER 3

It was a huge effort for me to adjust to my new job. I had come from a working environment that was all black, even though the ownership of WLIB was white. On my new job, everyone was white—even the janitors. The year was 1967, and things were far different from what they would become.

Many of the ABC people were less than ecstatic to see a black man on the staff, and some showed it. Racism? Of course. I had preconditioned myself to expect it, and I was genuinely surprised when people treated me well. Whites were learning that the old days of overt racism were on the way out. Some were acquiring new methods of hiding their racist attitudes. The tension at the station was double sided.

I had my hands full with the workload. I am not an extrovert by nature, and I was now in a business that demanded the very opposite personality from my own. Wherever I went to cover an assignment, I was exposed to a curious public. As soon as I arrived at a scene with my camera crew, we altered the atmosphere by the commotion we caused.

I also had to adjust to working in a visual medium, whereas my training had been in an audio environment. My work now had to be conceptualized in visual terms. An interview demanded that the subject be properly placed in front of the camera. The cameraman was responsible for getting the right visuals to illustrate the point of the story I was reporting. I was responsible for everything.

I grew to realize that a TV reporter is, in fact, a mini-producer-director. The reporter is in charge of the camera crew, and I had to learn how to deal with the personalities of these teams, all of whom were more seasoned in the business than I. Most were earning at least as much as I, and some resented having to take orders from a newcomer who was black.

I was assigned to cover stories that were far different from those I had reported at WLIB. The WABC-TV news department was all white except for me, and the priorities of what went on the air each evening reflected that equation.

At WLIB, I worked to assemble a newscast designed solely for a black audience. Everything was covered from this perspective. The assignment of stories was made by a black newsman, which was the reverse of the situation at WABC. The assignment editor was (and still is) white, and the type of stories he assigned to be covered consistently reflected what *he* thought was important.

People assume that the person who is seen on camera is in control of what he or she is reporting. But only three people in a TV newsroom have the power to decide what is to be covered and presented on the evening news report: the assignment editor, the producer, and the news director.

The assignment desk operates round the clock, and the assignment editor keeps a finger on the pulse of the news, locally, nationally, and internationally. The morning assignment editor is the most influential. The news report is based on what is running on the wires of the Associated Press or United Press International; what is in the morning newspaper; the flood of news releases that come in daily; what is broadcast on the radio that is kept tuned to WINS; the police radio broadcasts; tips; and other sources. The assignment editor decides what will be on the newscast and also decides which reporters will cover the stories.

The newscast producer usually arrives late in the morning and is on the job until after the evening news. The producer is totally responsible for the content, flow, attractiveness, and "newsiness" of the evening program. He or she passes judgment on what the assignment editor has delegated for coverage and has the authority to cancel stories, reassign people, or assign new stories. The producer has "final cut" regarding the content, balance, and writing of the stories.

After the reporter has covered a story, the producer assigns a writer to look at the videotape. The writer cuts the story into what is shown on the air. The producer judges whether it is suitable for viewing that evening, and he or she can alter or kill a story. The producer also decides what story will lead the newscast, which stories will fall at the end, and the stories' length and follow-up potential.

The news director has overall authority, although he or she is usually concerned with executive affairs of the department. She or he controls salaries, vacations, budgets, promotions, and hirings and firings. Occasionally, the news director supervises the newsroom. The news director hires both the producer and the assignment editor and wields the most clout. If the assignment editor gets into an argument with the producer about a particular story, the matter is settled by the news director.

These three people control what is seen by millions each day on the news. Who are they? Where are they from? Where are they *coming* from? What are their credentials?

The news director is usually an ex-producer. The producer is usually a former news writer or assignment editor. The editor is usually an ex-writer. They may or may not have a background in journalism. Most have had long careers in a working capacity in the news business and are quite capable. However, most are sadly

35

lacking in experience with a significant proportion of the racial population they are reporting to and about.

The population of blacks in the WABC-TV viewing area totals about thirty-five percent. Spanish-speaking people number about twenty-five percent and other "minority" racial groups represent about fifteen percent. I have never heard of a news director, producer, or assignment editor at any of the major radio or TV station news operations who are either black, brown, red, or yellow. Mass audiences are being subjected daily to information that comes from the priorities and preferences of a small number of people who represent less than half the population.

Can white people report and present news in a manner that is fair to blacks? Perhaps, but I ask: Would a white person accept a reverse situation, where the news was ninety-nine percent controlled by persons of color? The answer: Of course not. And whites would be justified.

The reporter does have *some* authority. A reporter can suggest story coverage to the assignment editor, the producer, and the news director. Reporters can fight to save certain stories from being killed and fight to kill other stories. There are, of course, several black reporters in the business today.* All, however, are subordinate to the authority of those who are not black. No blacks in the New York area in TV or radio or at news bureaus have "final cut."

On the network level, there is little that one can comment on regarding black involvement on a decision-making level. ABC stands out as being the only one of the three commercial networks that has a black anchorperson appearing regularly on the weeknight newscasts. Max Robinson delivers the news with

*"White males continue to constitute the great majority of all [news] correspondents, 82.2 percent.

"The networks should make training and placement opportunities in decision-making positions in their news departments available to minorities."

("Window Dressing on the Set: An Update," Report of the U.S. Commission on Civil Rights, January 1979.)

36

unquestionable authority and competence. However, ABC has no black involved in the decision-making level of the news operation. Several blacks are employed but on less powerful levels.

NBC has no black anchorpersons and never has had. No black journalist, to my knowledge, has ever delivered a commentary or analysis on the NBC nightly news. None of those who have prime influence over the content of the NBC newscast are black. On weekends, a black anchor has been seen from time to time, but anchorpersons seldom have any say about the content and context of the newscasts they deliver.

CBS has been dominated by Walter Cronkite for several decades. Cronkite is also the managing editor of his newscast, which means that he has considerable and often final control over the content and context of the broadcast he delivers. A number of producers work on the CBS newscast on a regular basis, and at least one is black. But all these producers are subordinate to Cronkite. They don't have final cut.

Ed Bradley has been doing the anchor spot on Sundays, and he is very good. He and I chased stories for our respective stations in the early seventies. We became quite friendly while staked out at a location waiting for an event or personality to "happen." Bradley started his career at CBS in radio. He has worked as White House reporter for CBS and was assigned to cover Jimmy Carter's presidential campaign. Ed has done two fine documentaries aired in prime time—a rarity. The first dealt with the boat people in southeast Asia, and the second took a look at how far the United States has come since the *Brown vs. Board of Education* Supreme Court decision of 1954. This last documentary was one of the few programs in which a black has examined black issues in prime time. But the producer of Bradley's newscasts is white.

An earlier CBS news effort dealt with the impact of movies on

37

racial attitudes in America, and the host was the excellent actor and comedian Bill Cosby. The producer, however, was white.

There are now many blacks on the news teams of New York, New Jersey, and Connecticut and in many other areas of the nation. I suspect that blacks on out-of-state local news teams play almost no decision-making role in the broadcasts, despite their prominent positions on the screen.

I soon found myself in the situation of being token black as a reporter with WABC-TV. The news staff was a fraction of the size it is today. There were only three reporters, and I was the third. Only four or five news crews operated, whereas today, Eyewitness News uses more than a dozen reporters and almost as many camera crews.

Initially I had some difficulty learning to make full use of the film medium—for example, cutting film for airing. Fortunately, my writing background was adequate, and I used my skill to reduce even the major news stories to air time of two or three minutes.

A number of solid newsmen worked in the newsroom when I joined the team, and they applied the pressure I needed to refine stories and cut them to a proper length. One day I was called into the news director's office and was told that they wanted me to audition for an anchor spot for the weekend news. An *anchor spot!* I was thrilled.

I had been with WABC only four months, though, and I was scared. It was one thing to be seen on TV as a reporter, with only the back of my head visible in the shots, and quite another to confront the camera "live" knowing that hundreds of thousands of viewers would be watching.

The dreaded fluttering butterflies of my early days returned with a vengeance. The audition was successful, and I started doing the late-evening weekend report in February 1968. I have been doing it ever since.

On the occasion of that first newscast, I came into the newsroom three hours before air time and went through the motions of going over that day's news stories. I was paralyzed with thoughts that everyone in town had canceled their plans for the evening just to sit at home and watch Gil Noble make a fool of himself in a fifteen-minute newscast. As the broadcast hour approached, my pulse rate increased proportionately. I may have appeared calm outwardly, but inside, I was quivering lemon Jell-O.

All too soon, it was time to leave the newsroom, script in hand, and head for the studio. From the way I dragged my feet, I could have been walking my last mile. Somehow, I found myself easing into the anchor chair—that same chair that held Bill Beutel during the week! The stage director gave me the traditional show business good-luck wish, "Break a leg!" and I heard the countdown to air time begin.

"Ten seconds to air. Five . . . four . . . three . . . two . . . one." The next voice I heard was a soprano saying: "Good evening." It was *my* voice, and I realized I was automatically reading the news copy without even thinking about it. In fact, I was so detached that it was as if I sat beside myself, observing, while I delivered the newscast. After what seemed to be one hundred years, the fifteen minutes had passed, and my pounding heart marked another hurdle in my broadcast career.

Tex Antoine was especially helpful during those early days. He explained that he never considered that he was addressing a mass audience. He always pretended that he was talking to a friend. I modified this idea and have used it since, mentally directing my delivery to one person.

Events had brought me to the strange and exciting position of being both a reporter for Channel 7 News and anchorman on the weekend report, all in a very short time. More was to come, because just around the corner waited my show *Like It Is.*

CHAPTER 4

Until the spring of 1968, the American Broadcasting Company's flagship station had never aired a program that had been conceived, controlled, and produced by a black staff member. I worked in WABC-TV's news department as a reporter, but there were still no black writers, cameramen, or secretaries.

On April 4, a bullet pierced the lower jaw of Doctor Martin Luther King, Jr., and stilled the heart of one of the greatest men our country has ever produced. Few black Americans cannot recall what they were doing at the moment they heard the news of the murder that tore at the nation's moral fiber. Even those who had lost faith in his tactics and differed with his philosophy bled for the man who had led so courageously.

I was in Harlem attending a meeting of black journalists when I heard of the assassination. At first I was shocked by the news—everyone was. We hoped he had only been wounded and not killed, but within minutes the word arrived that he was gone. We went out onto 110th Street, where people wandered aimlessly, approaching each other with a stunned, searching look in their eyes.

First they had killed Malcolm and then Martin. People said Malcolm had preached violence, which wasn't true, but it made it seem inevitable that he had died violently. But Martin Luther King's philosophy had been nonviolent, and he now lay dead with the other. Both leaders were assassinated in their fortieth year. Both were voracious readers and electrifying speakers. Both possessed great organizational skills and had expanded their analysis of racism to the international level. Obviously such threats to the American scheme could not be permitted to exist.

I had seen and interviewed Doctor King for WLIB and WABC-TV. I had heard him speak at the Convent Baptist Church on 145th Street and Convent Avenue and had been overwhelmed by his power. I have come to believe over the years that King's central thesis of morality was inappropriate—that he was preaching the right ethic to a system that couldn't understand because of its own inherent immorality—but although I criticized him, I cared about the man.

The next day at work someone in the newsroom said, "I'm sorry." America also appeared to feel sorry about Doctor King's assassination. A series of prayer vigils and prayer marches involved many whites. The Sunday following the assassination found Nelson Rockefeller linking arms with Charles Kenyatta to lead several thousand mourners from 125th Street and Seventh Avenue to Central Park.

In the ensuing months, several commitments and resolutions were made by American businesses and government to step up integration and "minority" advancement programs. Ed Silverman, the WABC-TV news director, announced that a decision had been made to create a black-oriented program. The actor Robert Hooks would be the host and interviewer. I was to add the news dimension. Meetings and planning sessions were scheduled over the next weeks, and it was decided that the program would be produced by the news director and written by Larry Goodman, the producer of the 6:00 P.M. newscast, and Al Ittleson, the newsroom assignment editor, both white. In late

April of 1968, the interview program was aired.

The original title selection had been *The Way It Is*, until Hooks and I argued for and got them to change it to *Like It Is*. The original theme music was rock 'n' roll, and we persuaded WABC to hire Jackie MacLean, a brilliant alto saxophonist and lifelong friend of mine, to compose and record a jazz theme. WABC-TV's first black-oriented show was underway.

A few months later, Robert Hooks left *Like It Is* to take a co-starring role in a new TV crime series called *N.Y.P.D.* He urged that I be given the job of host for *Like It Is*, although I really didn't think I was ready to handle it. I finally agreed to try, and the first of my shows aired as a one-hour interview with a panel of teenagers. The program was reviewed favorably by the *New York Post*.

The original format of *Like It Is* was essentially that of a magazine. There were usually a number of unrelated segments that focused on the minority condition. Toward the end of the year, the news director hired Charles Hobson, a black, as producer.

Hobson had been one of several producers who worked for the educational-television network's program *Black Journal*. He had been among a group of black producers who quit after a confrontation with WNET management about the program's content. Once he was affiliated with *Like It Is*, Hobson hired a small staff of blacks to produce the program, and was given office space behind the newsroom. I got along well with Hobson, although I saw little of him because of my full workload as a street reporter.

I attended several production meetings during the week, and we taped the show on Saturday mornings. Despite all the ballyhoo about the program's being black, until *Like It Is* was under our control, black it wasn't.

Hobson gave the go-ahead for staff member Elombe Brath to

43

begin assembling a documentary on Marcus Garvey. It stands today as the only one-hour TV documentary on this monumental black man.

I began to put together a documentary on the life of Malcolm X and was awakened to the existence of the WABC film vaults. As I spent hours going through films, I saw how Malcolm had suffered at the hands of the media, as had the entire black experience. The films made of Malcolm speaking at Harlem rallies, news conferences, and individual interviews were done mostly by whites, edited by whites, and presented by whites.

Mal Goode, ABC's first black reporter, did most of the interviews and coverage of Malcolm, but the editing of that film had not been done by Mal. The most relevant of Malcolm's statements were never aired. Mal Goode wasn't the only reporter to interview Malcolm X, but all the others were white.

Malcolm was stunning in his ability to answer reporters' questions, as though they had come from the lips and minds of children. It made me feel wonderful to belong to the same race as this genius.

I painstakingly incorporated as many of these rejected clips of film into my documentary as possible and contacted M. S. Handler, a white reporter at the *New York Times*, who had covered Malcolm's career heavily and fairly. Handler told me that Malcolm had taught him more about America and himself than he ever learned before.

I next decided to contact Malcolm's widow, Betty Shabazz. Betty had not granted any interviews of substance until that time, and I didn't know what my chances would be. I explained that I was compiling a documentary on her husband and asked if she would be available for a film interview. She was cool and said that she didn't think she could but that I should call her the next day for her answer. I made the call, and we discussed the interview once again. This happened for a week, until Betty began to

44

soften. One week later, she agreed and told me to bring my camera crew.

When we arrived at her home in Mt. Vernon, one of her children answered the door and showed us inside. I could feel Malcolm's presence immediately, especially from the magnificent oil painting of him hanging prominently in the living room. Betty entered smiling and shook my hand. We talked carefully as my camera crew set up lights and microphones for the interview. Betty was on her guard, and I felt intimidated by the entire experience.

By the time the camera crew was ready, I was more comfortable, and Betty introduced her six children. The two youngest are twins whom Malcolm never saw. Betty told me years later that Malcolm felt it had been prophesied that he would have six daughters before his first son would be born.

The eldest child, Attalah, looks exactly like Malcolm. Now an incredible young lady, she even cocks her head and pokes her forefinger into her cheek when talking, as Malcolm did. Attalah has a great sense of humor, and her mind is razor sharp.

The film I took during that day at the home of Betty Shabazz proved to be one of the most important aspects of the documentary. The audience was glad to see that Malcolm's family was all right.

Putting together my first documentary was a valuable experience, and my reporting background was an asset in producing this show. I had developed a sense of ethical balance, even though there was little of such consideration in the business that was evident to me. I added to the program ingredients learned from my people. I followed the edict of the country preacher and tried to "make it plain." I was not afraid to use colloquial terms and other of the spices that make language flavorful and give texture to the reports.

While I worked, I made mental notes of what I had seen in the

45

film archives of WABC and other archives in the New York area. Black scholars had long been aware that whites controlled the recording of black history in textbooks and newspapers. I was seeing that the same applied to electronic journalism. Reporters and writers, film editors and producers, all selected favorites among the black leadership and thus often created leaders who seemed most acceptable to their tastes and purposes.

As I observed the slanting of stories and the exaggeration of the negative aspects of incidents and personalities in the black experience, I determined that I would not do the same. At first, I was meticulous in trying to present nothing but the facts. Any personal observations were labeled "commentary." I also learned that it was far better if someone other than myself got my point across. Although I was angry at the editorial abuse blacks had suffered on film, I decided to be objective and do documentaries, rather than trying to "get even with" white America.

Contrary to the usual division of labor at WABC, I was writing the documentary, supervising the film editing, and doing both the interviews and the narration. Normally, each of these functions would be handled by a different person. The fact that I was doing the documentary for *Like It Is* made it easier.

I loved every minute of it. It was a privilege to sit in front of a Moviola film screen and get a *real* education from Malcolm. One interview stuck out in my mind as an illustration of Malcolm's quick thinking. He was questioned by a white reporter in an interview on the streets of Harlem about his alleged statements on the ill-fated atomic submarine *Thresher*. How could Malcolm be happy? the reporter asked. He was speaking of his fellow Americans. "Not my fellow Americans," Malcolm shot back. "If they were my fellow Americans, and if my people were treated as fellow Americans, I would have been sad."

It was amazing that reporters persisted in trying to "nail" Malcolm. In reel after reel of film, he was shown being pummeled

46

constantly, but the reporters returned to him repeatedly, no matter how badly Malcolm had verbally beaten them with his wits.

It was probably Malcolm's uncompromising indictment at the time, that all whites were devils, that was most painful for whites to deal with. "Surely there must be some exceptions. Surely all cannot be devils." There was a resolute campaign to discredit someone who would level such a painful accusation. The term *devil* must have struck to the heart of the matter for whites. There must always have been a lurking feeling, or realization, at some point in the history of America that whites *had* behaved like devils. Malcolm presented the same irresistible source of terror and fascination that the cobra has for its victim.

In contrast was the film footage on Doctor King, which was much more favorable. Doctor King's pronouncements of love for his enemies and his commitment to nonviolence could have been a welcome respite from Malcolm's blistering statements that he hated his enemies and would defend himself if attacked. Doctor King became famous for his "turn the other cheek" philosophy. The demonstrations he organized were well planned and structured, and the demonstrators were taught how not to hit back when attacked. They engaged in prayer when faced with physical harm, and even when women were assaulted by police, as the entire nation saw at Selma, the men refused to strike back. Priests were murdered, men and women were shot, churches were burned, and *still* the movement sang "We Shall Overcome."

CHAPTER 5

As my career developed, I found myself enjoying the beginnings of being a "celebrity." People stopped me on the street to ask for my autograph and to discuss other news personalities. Most of us dream of becoming a celebrity. As a kid, I hung out on the street corner with my friend Jackie MacLean (the now great saxophonist), and we fantasized about being "stars." We would dream aloud about being called after in public and followed after by people begging for autographs.

As it turns out, I have never liked being a "celebrity" and have always felt uncomfortable when strangers approach me in public. I'm basically shy, and I also realize that it is simply the awesome power of TV that makes anyone or anything widely known simply by showing the person or thing on the screen often. The myriad household names in our lives—the Jolly Green Giant, Crazy Eddie, Charley the Tuna, and so on—exist merely because we have been conditioned and mindwashed by TV. We have committed jingles and slogans to memory because of the media-saturation process. Even bad personalities have become famous because of the frequency of their appearance on television screens.

I have always considered these facts when people approach me, and I still do. I am not a Joe Humble or Michael Modest, because

I do offer some value in the work I perform. But there are many equally capable people around who are anonymous only because they haven't been given the visibility that I have.

As I became more widely recognized, I received many invitations to speak at school and church functions. I was frightened about speaking before large gatherings. It was easy to be in a TV studio doing a newscast with a few technicians and other familiar people; I could blot out the fact that I was talking to several hundred thousand listeners. They could see me, but I couldn't see them. When it came to walking out onto a stage or standing at a dais to address an audience in person, though, it was a different brand of hair tonic.

In spite of my shyness, I wanted very much to be in touch with people directly, and I wanted them to see that people in the TV industry were not really stars. I wanted them to understand the tremendously powerful instrument that shapes their opinions, ethics, morals, values, and lives.

I set out to attack my phobia against public speaking by addressing small groups and reading from written notes. I quickly found that although this method gave me the protection I wanted—the insurance against saying the wrong thing—it was just not effective. I gradually moved away from using notes and began to talk extemporaneously, which wasn't so difficult, since I always spoke on the same theme—the media and their message. The more I talked, the more assured I became, and thus, my delivery became more effective. Audiences were eager to hear from someone inside the media who was not afraid to tell the truth.

I don't rate myself now as a top-notch public speaker, but I have gained self-confidence, which stems from having something to say. I become nervous only when I am not certain of what I have to say. I never think about myself or how I am doing while I am speaking. I concentrate on my subject and thereby don't get uptight.

Public speaking has been beneficial to my audience and to myself. The inevitable question-and-answer period allowed me to tune in to what people had on their minds. It helped me to align my priorities as a reporter and a journalist.

Public speaking has also led me into teaching. As a result of addressing students at St. Peter's College in Jersey City, I was offered a position by William Gray III, then the head of the Black Studies Department and now a Democratic congressman from Pennsylvania, to teach a media class. I conducted this class for a year and found that the pressure of teaching was good for me. I broadened my knowledge of media by doing research to prepare for my classes. I read extensively about the origins of information distribution and discovered the history of my industry.

It was fascinating to learn that the press in Europe was owned or controlled by people of wealth and power who had·a particular reason for trying to influence public opinion. Early journals were paid for by the publisher, with no hope of investment recovery. The journals were not sold but were posted or given away in the streets. There were no ads, and therefore, the only gains to the publisher came indirectly. Political power and business connections were strengthened.

But long before Europeans were out of their caves, Africans enjoyed sophisticated civilizations with elaborate and efficient media. There were public debates and textbooks published in ancient cities like Timbuktu (no relation to the Broadway musical). Runners moved news through the villages and cities. Animals and birds were also used as couriers of information. There was also the legendary wandering minstrel who carried information across the continent. The African drum was and is a powerful communication method. Basically, media had the same premise and purpose in Africa and in Europe.

When the ·Europeans enslaved the Africans, the Africans' communication system had to be destroyed. Africans were forbidden to speak their native language upon arrival in America. Colonialists in early America passed laws in each state forbidding the use of the drum. With the destruction of this vital communications system, the African was more easily enslaved.

Slave owners tried to inject their values into the minds of the Africans in order to neutralize their rebelliousness. Religion was used as a tranquilizer, and early American journals read by slave owners devoted entire sections to the announcement of slaveholder meetings and advice on slave management.

Ferderick Douglass, the great black abolitionist, taught himself to read, ran away to the North, and began publishing his own newspaper detailing the evils of slavery. The impact was devastating and caused other abolitionists, some of whom were white, to also publish journals on the issue. On a street in lower Manhattan across from City Hall, John Russwork and Samuel Cornish published the first black newspaper in America, called *Freedom's Journal*. The opening sentence of the editorial in the first issue read: "We wish to plead our own cause. . . ."

Periodicals and journals published by whites far outnumbered those of blacks. It wasn't possible for many black publications to exist, for economic reasons alone. Toward the end of the nineteenth century, technological advances enabled newspapers to evolve into dailies.

Eventually, the telegraph and the telephone made faster, wider news coverage possible. Advertising by businesses was seen as a way to raise revenues and enable newspapers to reach large numbers of readers. The two media power groups merged their activities, and several newspapers were bought out by private corporations. Advertising was not the only incentive; the opportunity to influence the interpretation of the news by the public provided an incentive also. Editorial policies became more controlled by corporate owners who had other than editorial or journalistic motives and values. Public opinion was manipulated, and

52

some publication moguls, such as William Randolph Hearst, even entered politics.

Media then took another giant step with the invention of radio. Almost every American household had a radio, allowing citizens who never read a newspaper to fall under the influence of slanted reporting and editorials delivered on the air waves.

Commerical advertising became the crux of the economy of radio broadcasting. Radio empires were built and accumulated fortunes for several major corporations that invested in radio. The emerging mass media were controlled by a few people who, with the power of a microphone, could make or break individuals or an entire people.

Before radio hit the American market, the phonograph-record business was already a thriving, multimillion-dollar industry. Among the major record companies were Paramount, Columbia, and Victor, all three of which sold "race records," or music produced by black musicians and singers. The record companies viewed "race music" as lewd and lascivious, and the records were sold under the counter in many white communities and openly in black neighborhoods.

With the advent of radio, the record industry soured as Americans found it cheaper to buy a radio and listen to all the recorded music they cared to. Eventually, Columbia Records became part of CBS, and Victor Records became part of the Radio Corporation of America (RCA Victor), which spawned NBC.

Despite the role of race records in making America's big three radio (and later television) networks possible, they continued to ban black music. Even when it was considered "acceptable" for radio audiences, this music was performed only by white musicians, like Paul Whiteman, Al Jolson, and Vincent Lopez (who called his radio-broadcast music "decaffeinated jazz").

This history of the development of the media became part of the course I taught at Jersey City State College. I was honored to

53

receive a post as artist in residence at Seton Hall University in South Orange, New Jersey, in a dual appointment by the Black Studies Department and the School of Communications.

My teaching career came to a halt in 1975 when I became the producer of *Like It Is.* I had to take on the responsibilities of being an effective producer, without shortchanging my students, and I was forced to make a choice. I decided to concentrate on the show, hoping to send the message I wanted to deliver to a broader audience.

The bulk of my labor today for the American Broadcasting Company goes into *Like It Is* and is one of the most rewarding aspects of my life. The main source of my pleasure comes in the unglamorous research necessary to pull each show together. I love to dig up facts by poring through books, cross referencing, and searching through the dreary film archives. *Like It Is* has evolved into a primarily journalistic program. I made up my mind when I became producer to eliminate most of the entertainment and focus on more serious issues of the black experience.

Having once been a professional pianist, I have more than a passing love for the entertainment world. Everyone knows blacks can sing and dance. But blacks are also the descendants of one of the oldest civilizations and have made contributions to the world in the fields of architecture, medicine, agriculture, mathematics, astrology, and religion.

Black people are still not being given fair coverage by mass media. At least twelve percent of America's population is black, but less than one percent of the broadcast fare deals with blacks, and most of what is produced is controlled by nonblacks. Such inequities compel me to infuse as much serious and relevant information as possible into the program.

In order to ensure that I keep a finger on the pulse of what is happening in the daily world of my city's black population, I cap the end of my busy office day with a continuing round of activities as a member of the board of directors of a number of community-based organizations. I carry a heavy speaking schedule and meet regularly with community leaders, often picking up vital information and program ideas as a bonus.

An important aspect of these community activities is the criticism I receive from those I represent to the public. One reason I get around so much and try to be accessible by phone is that I remember how difficult a time I had getting through to many blacks in good jobs when I was struggling. Although I have been advised to let someone screen my calls and thereby make better use of my valuable time, I always try to keep my personal vow to *be there* for my people. I cannot cut myself off from the very people who fought to get me this job.

Dealing within the American Broadcasting Company is a fascinating exercise. ABC is a white-dominated corporation with all the biases and prejudices of America in general. In the many years that I have worked with and for this company, I have felt the same amount of racism as any black man or woman in this nation, working for any firm.

In the big outfits like ABC, the racism is subtle but lethal. My biggest gripe is with the broadcast product. ABC, like the other networks, has consistently turned out programming that validates whiteness and invalidates blackness. The networks present themselves to Americans as fair broadcasters, which they aren't.

In 1977, ABC made broadcast history when they aired the eight-part series *Roots*, based on the epic work by Alex Haley. The telecast was termed historic, largely because the ratings were good. It was also a version of black history that the whites who produced it (David Wolper & Co.) could live with, even if it was not, in my opinion, a fair representation of Mr. Haley's book; nor was it a fair representation of the holocaust of my people.

The film version of *Roots* was produced and conceptualized by whites, and the casting was done by whites. Small wonder then that the cast was composed of dancers, comedians, and singers, black *and* white, brought together to portray one of the most brutal chapters of history.

Can anyone imagine a football player being cast in the NBC film *Holocaust?* Hell no, and rightly so. It just isn't compatible with the gravity of the subject matter. Yet O. J. Simpson, Ben Vereen, and Ed Asner—a football player, a dancer, and a comedic actor—played important roles in the televised *Roots.*

I am saying that people who are nationally known as athletes, dancers, and comedians deprive audiences of the proper· set of mind required to portray the horrible story of the enslavement of a race.

In the screenplay of *Roots*, Kunta Kinte was kidnapped. When his father came upon his son's pouch in the sand, and realized he had been captured, he turned his face heavenward and called out his son's name. Then he returned to the village to tell his wife about the kidnapping. It seems to me that any father who learned that his son was kidnapped—especially by slave traders—would start out in full pursuit of the boy. There would be no rest until his son had been rescued or the father had also been captured or killed, especially since the family portrayed in *Roots* belonged to a village of *warriors.*

It is historic fact that there were several battles between Africans and slave traders, and slave ships were burned on the water by native warriors. This was not shown in the television drama, and in my view, the resistance to capture that was shown hardly paralleled the crime. And so, the attitude of the largest TV audience in history was further distorted regarding black history.

A further confusion in *Roots* was the character of the slave ship captain as played by Ed Asner, a comedic actor. This captain was depicted as a compassionate and guilt-ridden man; yet most slave-ship captains would seem to have necessarily, by the very nature of their trade, been at least enthusiastic about their work—enthusiastic enough to kidnap millions of African blacks for profit.

In some of the later chapters of the series, Lloyd Bridges of "Sea Hunt" fame plays a brutal racist who is caught and tied to a tree by a black man whom he had victimized. Although the black has a bullwhip in his hand, he doesn't use it. This absence of realism caused *Roots* to be far off the mark, as far as I am concerned. It would have been a totally different film if it had been produced and controlled by blacks with their heads screwed on right. It might not have done so well in the ratings, but it would have been closer to the truth.

The docu-drama *King* also falls into the same questionable category when it comes to the effectiveness of current black exposure in the media. This program was aired by NBC and produced and written by Abby Mann, who is white. Mann is quoted as saying that his show " . . . is the kind of film Martin Luther King wanted." The result is a major film about one of the greatest American people, who was in the vortex of a powerful and complex multifaceted movement that challenged and changed America. It seems to me that a black would have given a show about a movement that was essentially black, in which the key people were black, and the goal of which was a better way of life for blacks. That would have been more accurate. Yet the film story was concocted by a white person who was on the periphery of the events depicted.

Even aside from the docu-dramas, a wide range of programming lies about the black experience by omission and by inferring that everyone in America digs the American way of life. The victimizer is made to look like the victim, and the reverse. A normal, intact black family is rarely shown in the media. Blacks are depicted as being at peace with America and at war with each other.* Soap operas lie about whites and blacks; yet millions are captives of the daily installments of fantasy. It is wrong to see so many Americans involved in the problems of a fictional family while there is so much left undone in their own very real family lives.

Because of the caliber of broadcast fare, I made the determination to provide an alternative. This decision has met with some resistance. Some people in the black community told me they would like to see some "lighter" moments in our programs. Many whites have told me the same thing. But I have built up a staff that is now on top of one of the finest repositories of black documentary film in the nation.

We have turned out documentaries about black heroes and heroines and have produced series on black history that have been applauded. We periodically focus on Africa, past and present—the wellspring from which my people came. American blacks have been robbed of this awareness.

We engage the services of historians who serve as consultants. Many whites feel intimidated when anger is expressed on the program. Others mistake the speaking of truth for racism. Some in the company feel that Like It Is is a "hate whitey" program. I can count several instances where I have been advised to tone down the programs. I have been accused in letters from viewers of everything from atheism to anarchism. It has been suggested that I leave America, since I have so much criticism for the country and

*"Here we have George Jefferson: entrepreneur, black bigot, a splenetic little whip of a man who bullies like a demented overseer, seldom speaks below a shriek and worships at the church of ostentation. Would you like to live next door to The Jeffersons? Or consider the character J.J. on TV's Good Times: a bug-eye young comic of the ghetto with spasms of supercool blowing through his nervous system, a kind of Electra-Glide strut. 'Dy-no-mite!' goes J.J., to convulse the audience in the way that something like 'Feets, do your stuff!' got to them three decades ago. Then there is the character Ray Ellis in Baby, I'm Back: a feckless black creep who deserted his wife and two children seven years ago, one step ahead of his bookie's enforcers, and has now reappeared to make excuses and bedroom eyes at the wife. Ellis and the show's writers make much merriment at the expense of the sober, straight career Army officer courting the wife; obviously, he is a turkey." (Lance Morrow, "Blacks on TV: A Disturbing Image," Time, March 27, 1978, p. 101.)

its citizens. Years ago, management refused to allow me to show a portion of a documentary on narcotic addiction in which an addict plunged a needle into his veins. Today, such portrayals of the facts of life are normal TV fare.

CHAPTER 6

One of the blessings of *Like It Is* is being able to meet so many people who are in the heat of the battle for justice. At this point, I must take time to make reference to my very special friendship with Betty Shabazz. We met several years ago and have become friends. She knows all too well the great debt I owe to her late husband, Malcolm X. I am not sure, however, that she knows of the great debt I owe to her. Throughout the years, she has given me valuable advice. She has helped also by telling me things about Malcolm and things that he gave as advice and personally explained. He had come to understand many world issues, and his analyses still stand. I thank Betty for passing them on. Most important, she has helped me to discipline myself and learn to evaluate people.

Certainly, one of the most impressive men I have ever met is Michael Manley, prime minister of Jamaica. He is the embodiment of all that a leader should be. We met in 1976 when he consented to do an in-depth interview for *Like It Is*. We have met several times over the ensuing years, and I like and respect the man for his courage and integrity. He is not without fault, but I have never heard anyone question his integrity or his honesty. Manley is impressive in appearance and even more impressive in his intellect and ability as a speaker. He is one of the best-read men I have encountered.

Manley heads a nation in the throes of change. The struggle to unhinge the yoke of colonial rule and neo-colonial domination of the Jamaican mentality has been enormous. The Manley government has caught pressure and criticism from within Jamaica and without. An analysis of Jamaican politics comes later in this book, so let it suffice for me to say that Jamaica's prime minister is one of the outstanding individuals I have been privileged to meet. I wish him strength and courage for the many challenges in his future.

I have met other heads of state but have not come to know them as well as Manley. I interviewed Ahmed Sekou Toure, the president of Guinea, for *Like It Is*. Thus I got the opportunity to meet a man I have long admired for his politics and skill at governing his country. He has emerged as one of the few long-distance runners of progressive African leadership. I experienced some difficulty in interviewing him because he speaks no English and I speak little French. It is ironic that two persons of African blood had no common language to communicate with.

President Toure has visited the United States several times and has always distinguished each visit with a trip to Harlem. Although his awareness of the struggles of the Afro-American is not as sophisticated as some might expect, his effectiveness on the African continent is beyond question.

I have also enjoyed the opportunity of meeting and interviewing Sam Njomo, leader of the South-West Africa People's Organization (SWAPO) in Namibia, Kenneth Kaunda, president of Zambia, Joshua Nkomo, co-leader of the Patriotic Front in Zimbabwe, Leslie Harriman, former Nigerian ambassador to the U.N., and Robert Mugabe, the newly elected prime minister of Zimbabwe. All have appeared on *Like It Is*, and each has given insights into the complexities of the fight for liberation in Africa.

62

I have also met and interviewed several young people who are actively engaged in the African-liberation force. One such person is Tsetse Mashinnini, a student leader from Soweto, South Africa, who organized the 1977 uprising that became an international headline story. An intensive house-to-house search was conducted for Mashinnini, but in a beautiful show of solidarity, no one in Soweto knew where Mashinnini was, nor could anyone be found who knew or had even heard of him!

Mashinnini traveled to the United States to heighten public awareness of the real situation in South Africa. He was only nineteen years old when I interviewed him, yet was well informed on international affairs and aware of what his role in life should be within that spectrum. There was an unusual air of confidence about him, along with a maturity that supported his views. He shocked the TV audience when he stated that he hated white people, but as he talked of the brutal realities of white oppression in South Africa, who could blame him for feeling bitter and resentful?

In my opinion, it was good for the young people of this country to hear a youth speak from a completely different orientation and value system. Mashinnini had a burning purpose in life—to overthrow his oppressor. There was no space in his life for disco, television, or drugs. He was wrapped up, not in himself, but in the freedom of his people.

I also interviewed a female African teenager named Sededzai, a soldier in the army of the Patriotic Front in Zimbabwe, who operated a bazooka. She, too, was immersed in the fight for freedom for her people. We hit it off fabulously. Her way of calling me "my brother Gil" was totally disarming.

I asked both South African teens what their impressions were of the young people in the United States. They expressed sharp disappointment in the lethargy and apathy on the campuses they had visited. They were shocked at the amount of drug use. On the positive side of their impressions of America, they both had the greatest admiration for Malcolm X. Even with the severe restrictions on literature and information about militant leaders like Malcolm, word had reached these South Africans.

I met Stokely Carmichael for the first time in 1969 as the civil rights movement was dying. He generated electricity when he walked into the ABC studio with his former wife, Miriam Makeba, from South Africa. There were no blacks working in TV studios at the time, and the tension could have been cut with a knife.

Stokely was extremely bright and was about to embark on a long sojourn in Africa to study the works of African revolutionaries. He spoke of the role of Africa in the destiny of blacks in America, and named Kwame Nkruma of Ghana and Ahmed Sekou Toure of Guinea as heroes.

It was as though Stokely realized that black energy in America would diminish for a time and that the new upsurge would be in Africa. He had been among the first northern students to be excited by what black students were doing in the South in the fifties. He enrolled at Howard University in Washington, D.C., when he graduated from the Bronx High School of Science.

Stokely knew there was much organizing underway to build the potent Student Non-Violent Coordinating Committee in which he was to become a central figure. Even his marriage to Miriam Makeba had important political implications.

Miriam Makeba was the most prominent African artist on the international scene, and she was outspoken about what was being done to blacks in her country. Makeba was discovered by Harry Belafonte, who brought her to the United States and helped launch her career. There is hardly a piece of music in her repertoire that doesn't carry a message relevant to the struggle to end the racist domination of her homeland by Europeans. Stokely and

64

Taking a shot at a music career (1962).

My wedding reception in Moscow, U.S.S.R., August 1, 1959
—with Ambassador to Russia Llewelyn Thompson and his
wife. Best move I ever made.

After delivering one of my first speeches at the Union Baptist
Church in Montclair, N.J. (1969).

In the presence of a genius. "Duke" Ellington as he rehearsed for his second Sacred Concert at the Cathedral of St. John the Divine in New York.

The "Duke" died shortly afterwards.

My wife, Jean, and I accepting the New York Urban League John Russworm Award from executive director Livingston Wingate (1969).

Firing away at John Lindsay when he was Mayor of New York.

Groping for words upon receiving my fourth "Emmy" for my Harry Belafonte Special (February 4, 1979).

With Geraldo Rivera when we were co-hosts of *Like It Is* (1973).

With "Dizzy" Gillespie.

With Adam Clayton Powell
and Gene Simpson of
WCBS-TV News.

With the "greatest," Muhammad Ali, in 1976.

Interviewing Sidney Poitier
in 1978.

With the Patriotic Front's Robert Mugabe and Joshua Nkomo on *Like It Is* in 1978.

With Michael Manley in 1980, before the election in which Edward Seaga replaced him as Jamaica's leader.

With Harry Belafonte in his Manhattan apartment.

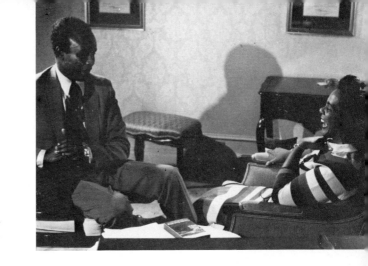

I must have amused Coretta King to evoke this much laughter.

At a UN reception with Organization of African Unity Ambassador Dramane Ouatata and his wife.

With (from left to right) Mal Goode, former ABC-TV news correspondent; Hon. P. J. Patterson, Minister of Foreign Affairs, Jamaica, W.I.; Tony Brown, TV journalist; Bill McCreary, WNEW-TV News; and Jimmy Booker, journalist and publicist.

Chairing a music panel discussion with **Dizzy**
Gillespie, Bobbie Humphreys, Reggie Workman
and Gil Scott Heron.

A group of students surround me while visiting
the WABC-TV live weekday program *Good
Morning New York*. At my left is Elombe
Brath, a staffer.

Makeba appeared together several times on *Like It Is*, he with his sharp analysis of the political situation in Africa and she with her musical political statements. Each time they appeared, the dedicated couple left *Like It Is* audiences with a valuable perspective of the African heritage.

In 1970, when Stokely and Miriam first appeared on my show, they were joined by H. Rap Brown. People of this caliber were beginning to hear that *Like It Is* provided a fair hearing on what was traditionally an editorially hostile network. Rap Brown is tall and thin. He was very quiet and polite during the show. I had taken my small son to the studio, and Rap picked him up, and they became fast friends for the day. Some nervous white employees in the studio were probably surprised at how gentle this "mad, raving brute" could be.

The truth is that many of our angriest activists were in fact quite humane. Few, if any, had records of violence. Rather, they were angry with America and had the guts to speak out. Rap Brown was vilified by national news media for suggesting that violence was "as American as apple pie." His words were prophetic as we all watched John F. Kennedy, Robert F. Kennedy, George Wallace, and others in the white sector of America fall.

Rap is supposedly now living in Atlanta. He is said to be a changed man. There are rumors that he was subjected to beatings and drugs while incarcerated. Prison subdues people, and incarceration is notoriously effective as a way to extinguish revolutionary fires. We can thank Rap Brown for raising a valid argument with white America.

In the latter part of 1978 I finally met and interviewed Eldridge Cleaver, former leader of the Black Panther Party, who was in New York promoting his book *Fire On Ice*. Cleaver had fallen from favor in the black community a number of years before, in part because of his denunciation of Castro's Cuba and partly because of his ties with other groups in America that many felt had no relation to black issues. Cleaver was impressive and exceedingly well informed. He had read almost everything relevant to revolution, and he spun an incredible story about the development of the Panthers and exactly how serious Huey P. Newton and the others had been. (At one stage, the Panthers were fully willing to confront the police and shoot it out. On many occasions they did just that. Contrary to press and police accounts, they only retaliated—they never initiated any violence.)

But Cleaver is no longer the same man who once captured national headlines. He has changed. Huey Newton has changed. Cleaver is now a "born-again Christian" and sells men's trousers that feature a separate pouch for the genitalia. He says America is the best place on earth. You figure it out.

Among the black activists I have known was Fannie Lou Hamer, a truly beautiful woman. Hamer died of cancer several years ago. Her funeral was attended by many factions of the civil rights movement in which she was so important. Militant and moderate stood shoulder to shoulder in a small church in Rulesville, Mississippi, to pay homage to a very great woman respected deeply by all.

When I interviewed Fannie Lou Hamer, she was still active. She had just been released from a Mississippi jail, where she had been beaten nearly to death and sexually molested by police. The beating was so severe that she limped for the rest of her life.

Hamer had become a marked woman because of her leadership in organizing sharecroppers and unions in the South. She also mobilized a voter-registration campaign. In 1964, she led the fight to get black Mississippians a participatory role in the Democratic National Convention in Atlantic City. Until that time, blacks from Mississippi had played no part in a Democratic National Convention. Hamer first tried to get blacks included in the Mississippi delegation to the convention. When that attempt was rejected, she formed the historic Mississippi Freedom Democratic

66

party (MFDP) and sought to have that group seated at the convention.

This challenge proved formidable in Atlantic City. The MFDP had their credentials in order, and there was no reason why they should not be seated; yet the leaders of the Democratic party maneuvered their way out of recognizing the organization. Even Hubert Humphrey failed to take the right stand on the matter. The MFDP was ejected from the convention. Out of this challenge, the Black Panther party emerged, making Mrs. Hamer's role a key element in black history.

I met Harry Belafonte in the early seventies. I had contacted him about appearing on *Like It Is*, although at the time I was not the producer and thus couldn't offer any assurances about control of the show's content editing. Belafonte was very gracious as he questioned me about the program during a meeting at his Manhattan office. He invited me to lunch at the Russian Tea Room. I experienced quite a rush, walking into that crowded posh restaurant with the famous Harry Belafonte!

He expressed uncertainty about doing the program and wasn't satisfied with the concept I had outlined. Those first meetings proved fruitless. He never actually refused, but the show did not materialize.

I continued to bump into Belafonte over the years, when he appeared at many of the political events I covered. One such occasion was a fundraising rally for Assata Shakur, a member of the Black Panther party who had been jailed, at least in part, for her politics. The rally took place in a packed Greenwich Village church. Many of those in the audience were obviously police agents. Belafonte acted as master of ceremonies and opened the program by speaking about the hypocrisy of the United States government—a government that professed to offer political freedom while denying that very freedom to many citizens. He spoke eloquently about the evils of oppression, racism, sexism, and other forms of exploitation. He used phrases such as *ruling class*. Belafonte spoke boldly before an audience that was heavily infiltrated by police and before TV cameras that would broadcast his criticisms to the entire country.

I was aware of Belafonte's long association with the civil rights movement of the sixties and knew that he was a close confidant of Doctor King's. He had given both time and energy to the movement, and thousands of dollars, as well. He used his personal friendships with many big stars of stage and screen to involve them in the civil rights struggle. During the historic march from Selma to Montgomery, Alabama, the singer arranged to fly a galaxy of entertainers south to boost the spirits of the marchers who were led by Doctor King. Many Broadway shows were canceled for a night to enable the stars to make the trip.

Belafonte made his apartment available for strategy meetings of the leaders of the civil rights movement during those tumultuous days of the sixties. I maintained my interest in getting him in front of the *Like It Is* cameras, and I finally succeeded late in 1978. The interview was filmed in Belafonte's Manhattan apartment. We filmed for nearly two hours, and all of the interview was so good that editing it was very difficult.

Regarding the interview, Belafonte issued no guidelines, although I would not have done the interview if any had been placed on either of us. He had a phenomenal memory and knew exactly where he had left off when we had to reload the camera. My show was the first extensive TV interview in which Belafonte could talk in depth about his life and values. I decided to extend the program beyond the usual hour. (Other extended *Like It Is* programs were "Martin Luther King, Jr.: An Amazing Grace" and "Paul Robeson: The Tallest Tree in Our Forest.")

The Belafonte interview started with a personal narrative about the singer's early life. He told of working as a janitor's assistant and receiving from a tenant in the apartment building a ticket for a play in a Harlem theater. Belafonte was nineteen years old, and it was the first play he had ever seen. The performance at the American Negro Theater transformed his life. He got a job with the theater company as an assistant stage hand, then worked his way into a small part in one of the company's productions and then into more important roles. Belafonte told of his transition into the world of singing—how he started as a pop singer in clubs like Birdland before he switched to folk songs.

I asked him how he had managed to keep his head when hit with the first flush of stardom. How had he dealt with fame, women, adulation, and wealth? He said that what had held him together were the strong values that had been instilled in him by his parents and by heroes like Paul Robeson. Thus, he had been able to keep his fame in perspective and use it as a tool to fight social injustice in the United States.

Belafonte talked about how he fended off the temptation of drug use. He disclosed his burning compulsion to be involved with the struggles of the oppressed—"gettin' it on," as he called it.

He discussed his role in the civil rights movement and talked about his close friendship with Doctor King. I used this connection by showing shots of Belafonte with Doctor King, and his orchestration of the Montgomery march celebrity night during the interview. Belafonte mentioned his relationship with Lester Young and Billie Holiday, and I included clips of both people. Much to my guest's delight, I surprised Harry with some film footage of him at twenty years of age. He was tickled!

Audience reaction to the Belafonte airing was stupendous. *Like It Is* was loudly applauded, and the Belafonte interview drew many viewers who tuned in just to see the singer. The singer himself called me to say that he had been overwhelmed by the positive reactions in his own circles. A deluge of mail poured into the *Like It Is* office at WABC. Most viewers wrote of their happiness in hearing such strong values coming from a man in

Belafonte's position. Others wrote to say how pleasantly surprised they had been to learn that Belafonte had so much depth beyond his performing talents. For the better part of the following year, Belafonte and *Like It Is* received raves over the two-hour special entitled "Belafonte: Looking Back."*

My friendship with two remarkable brothers from Detroit has brought one of the biggest dividends in my career. The Lee brothers stand out as impressive exceptions to my concern over the values of today's young people. They are serious, studious, and committed, while also being practical. The elder brother is in his early twenties, and the younger is in his late teens.

I met the Lee brothers by way of a telephone call from Detroit I received at my office. The caller identified himself as Paul Lee and explained that he was doing research on Malcolm X. I assumed that I was communicating with someone at least in his mid-thirties, especially when I realized that I was dealing with a person who had an uncommon amount of information about the available film on Malcolm. He explained that he had found his way to me through sources who had mentioned that I'd done several films on Malcolm. Paul quoted film clips and dates, and I immediately warmed to the conversation. He mentioned his plans to visit New York the next week and wanted to drop by my office. I agreed, looking forward to the meeting.

When Paul Lee walked into my office, I was shocked. This journalist-researcher, who I had assumed would be a mature thirty-five, stood in rumpled corduroy trousers, sneakers, and a sweater. Paul was eighteen years old. I recovered myself and asked how someone so young had developed a fixation on researching Malcolm X. Paul told me that while he was in his early high school years, he had heard one of Malcolm's speeches on a recording and had been thoroughly impressed. I told Paul that that had also been my way of introduction to the great man,

*In January 1980, the interview won an Emmy as best discussion-interview program.

70

and we recognized an instant similarity of viewpoints.

We talked for several hours, sparring at first like cautious boxers, testing the degree of knowledge each possessed. Then we went into my film-editing room, and I showed Paul some of the film on Malcolm I had gathered over the years. He sat watching the screen, mouthing the words as they came from Malcolm's mouth, so great was his knowledge of the leader. Paul was so familiar with the film clips that he even mimicked Malcolm's gestures.

I showed him the twenty-minute clip I had just acquired from England of Malcolm debating at the Oxford Union Society in London, a few months before he was assassinated. I was pleased to show this piece of precious film to a young admirer of Malcolm's. It was the beginning of a friendship that has continued over several years.

Later, I met Paul's older brother, Sunni (Carl), an equally serious youth, mature beyond his years. Despite the substantial gap between our ages, we have also become good friends.

Paul has continued to supply me with a steady stream of film and data on Malcolm. He produced the one tape recording of Malcolm's assassination at the Audubon Ballroom on February 21, 1965. I will use it in subsequent documentaries that include Malcolm. Paul has made trips to Washington, D.C., and spent hours in the Library of Congress and the National Film Archives, where he has uncovered newspaper clippings from several African nations reporting the impact of Malcolm's visits to those countries.

Although I sing his praises as a devoted young person, Paul is no angel. He dropped out of high school in his last year, but after a talk with me, he went back and got his diploma. He had become bored in school, but I convinced him that he needed an academic education. Paul went to college, where he again became bored, but he knows I would never come down hard on him just because he dropped out of school, provided he was engaged in an equally positive alternative activity. He has done just that by getting heavily into intensive research of the life of Malcolm X. I suspect that he will eventually return to school and do quite well.

Paul's older brother, Sunni, attends Howard University in Washington. Last summer, Sunni got a job as a staff assistant at the White House press office and thereby received fabulous exposure to one of the most sophisticated news and information centers on earth. Sunni and his brother will someday make a great contribution to our struggle as a people. This brother has steeped himself in African affairs and can speak of the many subtle aspects in the politics of the African-liberation movement.

Both young men come to New York often, and we sit in my office and talk for hours about the African situation. We discuss values and responsibility and the "now" generation. We talk about their home life, their girlfriends, their frustrations, their goals—just about every subject. It has afforded me a rare passport into the psyche of youth outside my own family members. We often discuss the civil rights struggle of the 1960s—both the gains and the mistakes that were made. I listened with interest as they debated who was greater, Malcolm or Martin. This has become a classic argument among blacks. I pointed out that we need both Malcolm *and* Martin in order to strive for unity within the effort to free blacks.

Through these two young brothers, I have seen the tremendous potential within us as black people. They have shown me the possibility that the coming generation will rise up and engage the forces of oppression in a fight. They are far ahead of me when I was that young.

Sunni is an orthodox Muslim. He is not affiliated with the Nation of Islam. He seems genuine and devout in his faith. He and his brother are courteous and abstain from drinking, getting high in any way, and smoking cigarettes. Whatever the Lee

72

brothers do with their lives, they will do it well and find a way to apply their values in a meaningful way as a weapon in the battle for the human rights of our people.

CHAPTER 7

Most of this nation depends on television news for information on what's happening in the world. Newspapers are still very much with us, but television is now the primary informing agent for contemporary society. People should learn to depend less on television news and at the very least, balance it with reading. This is because television news is centrally controlled, whereas newspapers are less so.

There are thousands of newspapers in America with different reporters, editors, and publishers, as well as conflicting pressures. Through newspapers, one has a better variety of news and better reporting. The thrust of the news in the *Washington Post* differs substantially from that in the *Christian Science Monitor*.

Television network evening news, however, delivers a carefully packaged newscast. For one half hour each night, Mr. and Mrs. America watch, transfixed and trusting, not considering the enormous number of world events that take place each day. They readily accept an antiseptic news sandwich that is twenty-two minutes thick, after commercials, and believe that they are well enough informed.*

*"Sixty to seventy percent of the people—polls seem to differ— say they get most of their news from television.

"That is disturbing. We in network news do a pretty good job, but in the attempt to cover the major events of the day in the limited time allotted to us, we are reduced, primarily, to a headline service. And you, of all people, know that the *full* story cannot be told in a headline."

(Walter Cronkite, April 25, 1979, before the American Newspaper Association convention.)

The people who put together TV news are a small nucleus who are overwhelmingly white, well paid, and opinionated. Most are also racially biased, to the degree that they cannot even accept that they are. If asked to share the awesome control over information with other ethnic groups, they reply that they're perfectly capable of reporting world events fairly and without bias.

I say it is impossible to be free of bias and American at the same time. It is in our collective blood, so why not make a variety of biases available to the public?

The wire services that supply the preponderance of news information are story-gathering agencies with bureaus all over the world. Their facilities to cover world events are much more comprehensive than any television station could afford. For this reason, all radio and television news stations subscribe to the wire services.

If the wire services don't report an international or a national event, television newsrooms across America will usually never know about it. This means that the viewer may never learn of it either. The wire-service bureaus are staffed by bureau chiefs and reporters. The bureau chief assigns reporters to news stories or news beats. Stories are filed daily, and if okayed by the bureau chief or person in charge, they go onto the state, national, or international wires.

The wire-service headquarters are in New York City, where a senior editor reviews the news and judges what is newsworthy— fit to be made known to the world. If the editor thinks a story is incomplete, he or she will wire the international bureau for more details. If the editor feels the report is not news, he or she kills the story. If approved, the story is readied for transmission to thousands of worldwide subscribers, including television newsrooms.

The story may be reshaped by the wire service before being sent out. Important pieces of information may be left out. Patriots can be redescribed as terrorists and vice versa. The bias of a big-city rewrite person can completely alter the complexion of a story.

Almost all the participants in the gathering and preparation of the news whom I have described are white.

Other sources of information include the *New York Times*, the secondary "Bible" for news in this country. If a story runs in the *Times*, news executives accept it as totally valid. If a story doesn't make it into the *New York Times*, many in the news business do not give it credence or air time. Unfortunately, the same standards of reportage cited regarding the wire services, including the racial imbalance among employees, also exist at the *Times*.

The selection of items slated for the evening newscast is made in the offices of the TV news executives, who are armed with these two major sources of biased information—the wire services and the *New York Times*—plus their own prejudiced attitudes and beliefs.

The following might be a bird's-eye view of a conference that takes place in one of those offices. "Let's not do any more on those rebels in Rhodesia. They've had enough play already." Or "Kill that Wilmington Ten piece, and let's just go with the Goldwater attack on Andy Young's statement on political prisoners."

At times the control is just that barefaced, and at other times it is more subtle. Each day, distinguished anchormen confidently gaze from television screens into the living rooms of millions of Americans and state: "Good evening, ladies and gentlemen. Here's what happened today."

These are not, for the most part, evil people. They are smart, educated, sensitive, and talented. Many will talk openly and with compassion about the problems of racism and exploitation. They can be heard to lament that they "just can't seem to find any capable blacks to hold the more responsible positions." They will have lunch with us and joke in the newsroom, so that on the

77

surface it seems that no war is being fought. But the combat against blacks, instigated by white politics and opinions, prevails.

Other factors influence TV programming—profits, for one. Along with the inbred desire to protect the white image and interests, is the desire to make money. This is the bottom line on which TV news is based. There is often more than a casual connection between personal interest and moneymaking. Some news stories are no more than promotional pieces.

When ABC ran the film version of *Roots*, the news department assigned a reporter to do a series of reports that were principally interviews with members of the cast. These "reports" ran just before the film aired. Alex Haley's book is a major literary event, worthy of news coverage because of its impact, but I question a news department's spending valuable air time interviewing LeVar Burton for a *newscast*. It seems a juxtaposition of values, mixing corporate gain with world events.

News departments of the major stations now utilize the services of consulting firms, which advise on how to improve the broadcasts and, therefore, the ratings of shows. These companies appraise the reporters and anchor people for popular appeal and may recommend that a certain reporter do a specific type of story that seems to best fit his or her "image." These consultants are neither news people nor journalists; yet they influence the presentation of television news.

These consulting firms also influence hiring and firing in the stations and even the running time of news stories. No story should run longer than two and one-half minutes, they state, because viewing audiences will become bored beyond that. They may switch channels! Reporters are often hired for their cosmetic qualities rather than their journalistic qualifications. Some reporters have been sent to drama coaches to heighten their charismatic projection and their appeal to audiences. News programs have become a popularity contest with the public, rather than a serious dissemination of the news, as they could and should be.

In addition to the money spent for such theatrical concerns, exotic budgets are assigned to concoct *Star Wars*–like sets for the news. One such was created by a Broadway set designer; another cost a quarter of a million dollars to build. Is this necessary to the purpose of the newscasting service?

Reporters are called into the news director's office with increasing frequency and are criticized on such vital points as their wardrobe, their makeup, and the need to smile at the camera more often. News teams are currently popular, since the consulting firms found teams to be most effective with audience ratings. The motivation behind these concerns is not to provide more and better news service, but to impress the viewing public.* It is not uncommon to hear of reporters who have been hired because they possess a certain "kinky" quality.

Newsroom executives have told me that reporters must become more involved in the stories they cover. We are to be visually prominent in film and taped reports, even if it takes more time to set up the camera crew to record the reporter striding into and out of a news clip. The results of this dictum are shown with the wasted footage of a reporter leaping from a car onto a scene and bouncing into a building.

Consultants have determined that audiences like newscasts that are delivered by teams of reporters who relate well to one another and joke openly on camera. It has also been determined that people will watch if the newscast includes a light story. These stories are called kickers. They range over subjects like a panty raid at the White House or a worm-eating contest in Peoria.

*"One of the great problems in TV news is lack of air time. That's why we're superficial and shallow. We let a lot of good things go by the boards simply because there isn't enough air time.

"Too many daily papers and magazines have picked up television's worst habits, and are using the same news consultants, to increase their circulation.

"Jazzing up the news is almost the worst sin. I can't support happy, tabloid news. . . . That kind of news goes against everything I believe in."

(Richard S. Salant, vice-chairman, NBC, former president of CBS News.)

They are designed to pick up the viewer's spirits and cause laughter. At one time in broadcasting, the lighter side was presented with the sports and weather, but now laugh-provoking material is liberally sprinkled throughout the news as well.

Television news is big business. To keep profits perking, stations publicize and promote news shows in the same way that advertisers sell soap. Stations spend hundreds of thousands of dollars on promo commercials to sell news personalities and teams. Space is purchased in newspapers, toward the same end.

The news people do not complain of this distortion. Their income levels have now risen to glorious heights, and some news people enjoy as much popularity as movie stars. They are seen more often and by more people than most movie actors and actresses. Some television news people are rich because they are trusted—whatever that means—although no one has ever told me why. Some newscasters are popular for their abrasive or obnoxious characters. One newsroom brought in a tailor from California to custom design a wardrobe for every reporter.

Many serious reporters have become confused and disoriented. The values of journalism they worked long and hard to perfect are no longer their most marketable commodity. They find themselves with colleagues who are not well equipped but *are* charismatic. Viewers often say that they like a particular station because the newscasters "seem to be having so much fun." Few in the audience complain about defective journalism or even want to discuss the news. They are interested in being entertained, being charmed, and having fun.

This brand of popularity helps to pay my salary, but there is a higher priority. I believe that the news has a primary responsibility to provide information, and since TV news has become the dominant source of disseminating information, we need a revised set of values to work under. I am certain that many of my fellow reporters would agree. Some have already spoken out, while others remain silent and simply collect their checks.

I have thought deeply before writing this indictment because I have a family and bills to pay, just like any other job holder. I know that I risk hobbling my career by speaking out. However, my job *resulted* from the struggle of my people declaring their feelings about the racial injustices they have suffered, and if not for the sacrifices they made, I would not now have this opportunity. I feel I have an obligation to speak the truth as I see it.

The need for improved news quality is great, and the lack of it falls far most heavily on blacks. Whites do suffer when TV news is less than it should be, but I think that the worst effects are made upon my people. The health of the black community is intertwined with the health of good communications. Both *community* and *communication* have the same root, and for good reason. If the proper values and information are not communicated, a healthy community cannot exist.

For example, in 1977 New York was hit by a massive power failure. The lead story from the '77 blackout was not the power failure, however, but the looting that went on in the ghetto areas. The term *looting* was emblazoned across the special TV news editions. The word scorched the covers of news magazines. And who were the looters? Black people. America was outraged. "Just look at those people! Why, they are just a bunch of animals, looting their own neighborhoods, their own stores!" Panels of reporters went on television the next night to discuss looting. Police were praised for rounding up the "animals" and throwing them into detention cells. Many of the looters stayed in jail for as long as a year without ever coming to trial.

I condemn looting, yes, but I also criticize mass media for indicting only certain looters, when there are other types who are never identified as such. Looting is not alien to Americans. It is by that process that this country was started. Europeans came to this continent and looted land from the Indians, but our "founding fathers" are never called looters by the media. These same European looters needed labor for their farms and sailed to Africa to loot that country of my ancestors, depriving them of their freedom, liberty, and dignity and denying them the basic human rights. The blood that courses through my veins was subjected to the most despicable deeds. The African slaves were unpaid, working from dawn to dusk with recompense looted from our lives. Throughout the history of this nation, the primary looters have not been pointed out. We have seen looting by police, mayors, governors, senators, congressmen, vice-presidents—even the figurehead of our government—again and again, yet without acknowledgment.

It was right for the media to condemn the looters in Brooklyn during the blackout of '77, but it is also right then to condemn the looters from 1619 onward. This unfair and imbalanced identification confirms ancient prejudices and biases.

Soon after the blackout came the issue of the Bakke case in the area of education. Mr. Bakke, a white student, sued a California medical school on the grounds that he was denied admission to make way for a black student with lower grades. The school had a racial quota to fill, which caused Bakke to be refused. A shout of indignation went up throughout the country as the public sympathized with Bakke and his complaint that he is the victim of "reverse discrimination." The open-admissions plan, which is only a few years old and was designed to give black students a chance to catch up after centuries of oppression and neglect in education, has now been called unfair.

In my view, mass media and television news in particular, have not been helpful in clearing up the confused values. Commentaries and editorials have tended to side with Bakke, and public opinion has thus been molded and a deep-seated resentment has bubbled to the surface. Many whites have resented all the programs for black advancement that were begun in the wake of the civil rights movement. They oppose anything that tries to move my people into better positions in this country, whether in jobs, housing, or education. Now these people have surfaced and are loudly denouncing the affirmative-action programs.

The years of abuse and deprivation that my people suffered are forgotten. We are supposed to catch up in a race that we never had an equal start in. Any consideration to a person so handicapped is ordinarily viewed as discriminatory. Are those in a hospital waiting room justified in telling emergency cases brought in with critical injuries to wait their turn? The news media could have given a completely different portrayal of the Bakke case and instilled another viewpoint in the public mind.

An area of newscasting that must be discussed is the relationship between white reporters and black communities. There are many instances in which the wrong side of a story is presented when it is what is termed a "Third World-community" story. This happens because most reporters don't know any better.

I do not say this with malice. A reporter is under powerful pressure to produce a compelling story in a short time. Often the reporter must write three and four stories in a day. Many stories involve communities, people, and lifestyles totally alien to the reporter's experience. He or she may see and hear things that divert attention from the real story.

A reporter can also turn a side issue into the focal point of a story merely because of her or his own limitations or bias. Reporters in quest of a story who cannot gain entry to a premises often focus on the fact that they couldn't get in, rather than on the event in question. Fights on camera have occurred this way. They are exciting to watch, but they nothing to do with the story in progress. Just because a reporter is not allowed into a premises does not mean that anything wrong is taking place there. But the intense pressure on a reporter to bring in a "good" story causes other than newsgathering to take place. If the story isn't "newsworthy" it reflects poorly on the reporter and the assignment editor who sent him or her out. New departments spend a lot of money getting reporter, camera crew, and equipment to a location, and they want something tangible in return. I have heard many assignment editors praise a reporter who can be depended on to deliver a story, even when there is no story to deliver.

All these elements make for tension and excitement in a newsroom. As the broadcast hour approaches, tension builds, the pace quickens, and the noise level elevates. Tempers grow short as staffers pour every ounce of energy into their contribution to the newscast.

The producer, who is responsible for the look and flavor of the entire package, suffers the greatest pressure. He or she must orchestrate the timetables of evey story and see that the show is ready on time. The producer also is aware that good journalism is not the only standard by which success is measured. In fact, bad journalism may be the least likely cause of criticism from upper management.

Writers are hounded by the producers for well-written stories delivered on time. Film editors are pressured to cut their film expertly on deadline. The newsroom often resembes bedlam. I am also caught up in the confusion, and then I wonder whether any of it makes sense. I question whether I am really a professional, no matter how successful or popular I have become.

CHAPTER 8

At the start of the 1950s, television was still in its infancy. Television news was considered a necessary evil, and the stations were required by law to devote a quota of air time to public-service programs. In those days, the news was presented reluctantly, almost as a ritual afterthought and in a drab manner.

Working journalists were employed either by newspapers, magazines, or radio. No self-respecting reporter took television as any more than a passing fancy—making a fancy pass at making a buck. Many TV network stations compelled reporters and announcers from their radio operations to also work on TV newscasts.

John Cameron Swayze was a radio staffer when an announcer was needed to work in the television end of the business. Everyone, including Swayze, refused the opportunity, but straws were drawn and the veteran announcer lost. Thus, one of America's best-known TV faces got onto the small screen by default.

It was a long while before journalists took television seriously. Television news moved to a more respectable and important position with the civil rights movement, beginning in 1954. When Rosa Parks, a hardworking seamstress, refused to give her bus seat to a white passenger in Montgomery, Alabama, her arrest triggered off one of the most explosive and dramatic news stories of this century.

Apart from the world wars, nothing has ever received the coverage given the ensuing rise of the black liberation movement. News teams from every corner of the nation converged on the South to report on what was growing and, in the process, made heroes and heroines of many ordinary people.

Stations had to acquire adequate equipment and personnel to send south to cover the story, and TV networks hired scores of reporters and technicians. For many news people, it was their first opportunity to meet black people. Conditions were tumultuous and even dangerous. As the struggle moved into the 1960s, it changed from a nonviolent movement to one in which new leaders called upon blacks to defend themselves if attacked.

As the movement continued and the nation seemed unable to find ways to solve the grievances of my people, the temper of the struggle changed, and there were explosions called riots. The major cities of America were racked with an agony of bloodshed and flames. Whole neighborhoods were reduced to rubble.

Television news reporters and camera crews were sent to cover these situations and were often badly intimidated by what they encountered. Not only were they in physical danger, but they were also subjected to a good deal of harsh verbal abuse. Unlike the genteel, conservative, loving manner of the civil rights leaders of the Southern Christian Leadership Conference (SCLC), led by Doctor Martin Luther King, Jr., blacks in the central and northern cities called whites honkies and crackers. They called police pigs. There was talk of revolution, and many of the groups appeared to be paramilitary.

The television industry was young and faced with a terrifying revolutionary situation. The trauma of those days has never left the memories of those in the front lines. Many reporters still strongly loathe an assignment in the black community. There are

86

often alibis and resistance when an editor tells a reporter that she or he is being sent to Harlem.

There have been times at news conferences in black communities when I've heard many insensitive questions asked. Reporters refer to those being interviewed as "you people," and they ask provocative questions, such as: "If your demonstration gets no results, will there be a riot?" Reporters and camera crews have intruded on funerals and have broken into private homes, and afterward solemnly reported the "violence" of which they themselves were the instigators.

Several star reporters have asked black leaders and groups at news conferences if they hate white people and if they believe in violence. Reporters have directed cameramen to film a group of showboating kids and then weave the footage into the story to give it a violent tone. One reporter goaded a group of young people into performing a yelling and cursing match at his cameras. Film editors in the newsroom love this kind of "action" footage, whether it is germane to the story or not. Television news moved from being a poor stepchild of the industry to a major source of revenue largely by covering the struggle of my people, and the news continues to pursue the same exploitative slant on racial subjects that brought them so much profit.

If this cycle can be broken, it will be by television news-assignment editors, who should be escorted through black communities to meet with people on an unofficial basis. Better yet, let a percentage of the assignment editors be black. In the New York area, which is the nerve center of TV news, there are no black assignment editors, black news directors, or black producers of TV news programs. Blacks may be serving in an "assistant" capacity, but none have ultimate authority in these three key job categories.

Certain dimensions of the black community, such as its positive values and achievements, seldom get aired. Even some blacks, especially children, believe the stereotypes they are fed, rather than the reality.

Harlem is one of the oldest and largest black communities in America. Mass audiences have a negative overall impression of this community because of a cascade of stories presenting Harlem as a ghetto, a slum, and a crime-ridden wasteland.

What, I ask, has been said about Harlem the mother of some of the world's finest citizens, such as Countee Cullen, Langston Hughes, Art Tatum, W. E. B. DuBois, Arthur Schomberg, Paul Robeson, Harry Belafonte, Ossie Davis, Sidney Poitier, Marcus Garvey, Malcolm X, and scores of others? What about the Harlem that produced some of America's most significant culture? What about decent people of Harlem who love, respect, work hard, and seek unity? It seems that these elements do not make exciting news copy.

Many say that the mass media don't want to show anything positive about blacks because that would compromise the self-esteem of many whites who base their sense of superior importance on the subjugation of other people.

Reporters should stop approaching black communities as if they were leper colonies. If only more of my colleagues would recognize that blacks in America are the victims, not the victimizers, we could straighten out this confusion and inequality.

Another inhibition to a healthy relationship between reporters and blacks is the bond that exists between newsrooms and the police. The police departments of this nation are assumed to be essentially on the side of good and to be trustworthy. Most of the stories covered in black communities involve the police, and since the police are trusted more than the members of the black community, blacks suffer.

When a reporter arrives at the scene of a disruption or crime, he or she usually feels most comfortable interviewing a police spokesperson to get the details of the story. Rarely is a member of

88

the black community asked for an impression of the incident. Every reporter should acquire a reasonable distrust of the police and go into the community, as well, to gather news information for a well-balanced picture.

The Attica incident, for example, is a case where the police lied to the press, yet were exclusively consulted for the details. Rebelling prison inmates, who were justified in protesting, were accused by police as having slit the throats of their hostages.

In the Knapp Commission report, scores of police revealed that they were on the take, and some were found to be selling drugs instead of arresting the pushers. Certain narcotics officers of the Treasury Department are widely known in black communities as having several drug pushers working for them under threat of arrest if they don't cooperate.

A book called *Search and Destroy* revealed the complicity and direct involvement of several murderous police officers in attacks on members of the Black Panther party. Facts show that the bullet holes in the Chicago apartment in which Panther leader Fred Hampton was killed came from outside. The police lied when they said they fired on the Panthers in self-defense.

Police have shot down and murdered hundreds of black youths; yet no police officer has ever gone to jail for this. One officer killed a Brooklyn teenager and was exonerated on the grounds that he had suffered an epileptic seizure that caused him to pull the trigger and afterward walk to his prowl car and report what he had done. The Patrolmen's Benevolent Association in New York City has recently been in the news complaining bitterly about a hospital doctor who had treated a mortally wounded suspect before attending to a police officer in less serious condition.

If only the news media would report on the police as the black community has seen them. As a youngster, I watched police officers drop by my father's auto-repair shop at Christmas to wish him happy holidays, extending their hands with broad expectant grins on their faces. My father told me that if he didn't have a bill in his hand when he shook theirs, he would be blitzed with traffic tickets.

In the late 1960s, it was not uncommon to see police officers in the newsroom examining film without subpoena. Several news people fed information to local police and FBI on many civil rights organizations and members, without subpoena. In fact, a WCBS-TV assignment editor was a former New York Police Department official.

Many police agents worked as reporters for organizations, as Richard Salant of CBS admitted recently. The international counterpart of the FBI, the CIA, continues to have several agents working internationally under the cover of being news reporters. This is done with the full cooperation of the news agency for which they work. Additionally, they manipulate news reports on what is going on in many Third World nations.

Early in 1980, John Hersey, president of the Author's League, addressed the Senate Select Committee on Intelligence in a letter with the following request:

> The national intelligence act . . . should unequivocally prohibit the C.I.A. (and other agencies) from using journalists and professional authors of books and magazine articles to gather information or perform other intelligence services. . . .
>
> The fact or the possibility that some journalists and authors may play a dual role as C.I.A. retainers can discredit other writers, have a chilling effect on their potential sources of information, and erode confidence in the United States press both here and abroad.*

I have acquired several documents from the files of the FBI under the Freedom of Information Act, and what I have read is both depressing and frightening. There are memoranda from agents who had infiltrated black communities and organizations

*C. Gerald Fraser, "Authors Ask Ban on CIA Ties," *New York Times*, March 7, 1980.

90

which spell out the weaknesses of the organizations and how best to destroy them. The Nation of Islam in particular was infested with FBI and local police agents whose mission was to undermine the organization by spreading rumor and fostering fights among the leaders. One memo detailed how the future direction of the Nation of Islam could be manipulated:

SAC, Chicago (157-2209)   January 7, 1969

Director, FBI (100-448006)

COUNTERINTELLIGENCE PROGRAM
BLACK NATIONALIST—HATE GROUPS
RACIAL INTELLIGENCE
(NATION OF ISLAM)

Although the Nation of Islam (NOI) does not presently advocate violence by its members, the group does preach hatred of the white race and racial separatism. The membership of the NOI is organized and poses a real racial threat. The NOI is responsible for the largest black nationalist newspaper, which has been used by other black extremists.

The NOI appears to be the personal fiefdom of Elijah Muhammad. When he dies a power struggle can be expected and the NOI could change directions. We should be prepared for this eventuality. We should plan how to change the philosophy of the NOI to one of strictly religious and self-improvement orientation, deleting the race hatred and separate nationhood aspects.

In this connection, Chicago should consider what counterintelligence action might be needed now or at the time of Elijah Muhammad's death to bring about such a change in NOI philosophy. Important considerations should include the identity, strengths, and weaknesses, of any contenders for NOI leadership. What are the positions of our informants in regard to leadership? How could potential leaders be turned to neutralized?

The alternative to changing the philosophy of the NOI is the

91

destruction of the organization. This might be accomplished through generating factionalism among the contenders for Elijah Muhammad's leadership or through legal action in probate court on his death. Chicago should consider the question of how to generate the factionalism necessary to destroy the NOI by splitting it into several groups.

Another memo concerned the impact Malcolm X was having on young people and warned that he was becoming far too attractive and influential. In light of these government memos, questions arise about the arguments and eventual split between Malcolm X and the head of the Nation of Islam, Elijah Muhammad.

There is also documentation that reveals that the FBI did not begin its surveillance and undermining of black leaders and organizations in the 1950s and 1960s. As far back as the 1920s, J. Edgar Hoover assigned agents to work undercover to undermine the enormous movement that had been assembled by Marcus Garvey.

Garvey had formed the Universal Negro Improvement Association (UNIA) during this period, and millions of American blacks joined it. J. Edgar Hoover monitored Garvey's activities and tried to catch him in wrongdoing and convict him (without foundation) and also attempted to influence his followers to forsake him.

The heavily financed effort succeeded, and Marcus Garvey was discredited and deported, forced to die in exile in England.

Doctor W. E. B. DuBois was also closely watched by the United States Justice Department during the late 1920s because of his criticism of American racism and his declaration of the need for a more socialistic form of government in this country. DuBois eventually joined the Communist party, and he, too, was attacked and discredited and forced to leave America, to die in Ghana.

One of the truly great and gifted men of this nation, in particular black America, was Paul Robeson. He was a brilliant actor,

92

singer, scholar, attorney, labor activist, anthropologist, musicologist, and linguist and an outspoken and militant fighter for his race.

Robeson rose to international fame and acclaim. America was proud of Paul—until he began to attack this country for lynching and brutalizing the black race. Robeson refused to be tricked into allowing the influential people to set him up as an example of how well blacks were being treated. He repeatedly lambasted racism and oppression in America. He pointed to the Soviet Union, where he felt there existed a system of government that had a greater capacity and willingness to be fair to all people and economic classes.

Robeson was vilified, and his lucrative concert and film career was brought to a standstill. He was denied access to the stage; his radio appearances were canceled. Paul Robeson never appeared on U.S. television. Two documentaries were done on Robeson toward the end of his life, both by black producers. The first was done for the educational network by Tony Batten, and I produced the second for WABC-TV.

Law-enforcement agencies were not content to stifle Robeson's ability to work in America. He was denied the right to work overseas by having his passport withheld for eight years. One official reason given for the suppression of this man was his criticism of the American government while he traveled abroad. His loud support of the liberation movements in Africa caused FBI offices across the nation to track Robeson and everyone associated with him.

I have personally seen several FBI papers on Robeson. These documents show that an extensive and well-orchestrated surveillance of this man was carried out over several decades. Only because of his incredible strength of body and character did he withstand persecution as long as he did.

Doctor Martin Luther King, Jr., one of the most pacific of men, who went so far as to say (and prove) that he would not defend himself if attacked physically, was hounded by police and FBI agents with a vengeance. America witnessed the recent assassination hearings on his murder, but police and FBI involvement was hushed. Doctor King *was* harassed by police agencies, and it is reported that the FBI sent him a letter saying that they had "the goods" on him and recommending that he commit suicide.

My own private investigation of the assassination of Doctor King revealed that the FBI, which watched his every move for years, had pulled out of the vicinity of the Lorraine Motel on the day he was shot. A team of FBI and Memphis police agents who were assigned to protect Doctor King were pulled off the job shortly before the rifle bullet ripped through his lower left jaw, throat, and neck. No one has ever explained why this protection was eliminated, and few have inquired.

My qualified respect for and trust of the police has carried over into my professional work. The essential role of the reporter is to be questioning and not gullible. More of my associates in the business should join in questioning the police when it comes to covering black-community stories in particular.

Protests from the black communities about the influx of narcotics were ignored, and now narcotics are in *every* community. America has long ignored police abuse of blacks for decades, if not centuries, with the result being police brutality against other groups of citizens. Police rioted in Chicago during the 1968 Democratic National Convention and battered scores of white youths. National Guard troops panicked at Kent State University and killed four white students. How long will such injustices continue to be ignored where they start—in the poor black communities of America?

CHAPTER 9

Malcolm X continues to dominate my thoughts and deeds, though in unexpected ways. Malcolm held many principles that I have adopted in order to improve myself.

First, he was a believer in punctuality. This may seem a trivial thing, but it has now come to mean a great deal to me. Punctuality is a standard in the *Like It Is* office. It has been good discipline for the staff and me to be on time, and it builds a secure sense of responsibility needed to cope with the urgencies of the times and our business.

Malcolm was a passionate reader. I was never turned on to reading during my school years, but I have developed my facility for reading because there is now a purpose to it. Reading has helped me become more effective at what I do. Reading can help anyone, no matter what they do. Through this means I can find people in history who had similar problems to mine. Studying how these individuals solved their problems helps me to solve my own.

As my knowledge has increased, my ego has decreased proportionally. Knowledge is the mother of humility and makes one realize how little is really known overall. Some people have misused knowledge by studying how to perfect ways to enslave and

95

dominate others. To overcome these people, one must be equipped with more and better knowledge.

Malcolm's deep interest in Africa impelled me to learn of that continent, what has been done to it, and at whose hands the exploitation was committed. Malcolm's influence encouraged me to become aware of my African descent, as did the influence of many other concerned blacks, such as Robeson, Powell, Du Bois, and Garvey.

Africa is the fundamental element of my being. The more African I feel, the more effective an American citizen I become. Because I have a sense of what I am, I am not willing to accept anything less.

I had been raised to think of Africa as a foreign land, peopled by strangers. I was never impressed with the fact that my bloodline went back to that continent. I was ignorant of the positive achievements Africans have produced. I had never been told of Imhotep or the great wall of Zimbabwe. I had never been told that iron was smelted first in Africa or that Africa possessed great wealth in natural resources. Many white Americans were also deeply interested in Africa, but I as a descendant was kept in an ignorant state. I didn't know that America had been party to the colonization of Africa, and I never understood the full meaning and dimension of slavery.

Malcolm taught me about manhood, as well as history, and showed in his own actions that male pride and maturity were not a condition of muscle or sexual prowess, but of character, commitment, and the courage to give up everything in order to be free.

Malcolm showed me that if one fought for one's race, respect and some assistance would come from other quarters. I learned that to refuse to fight the criminal only condones the crime. Many outside of my race have supported the stands I have taken in the work that I do for my people. I fall short of the values that

Malcolm exemplified, but nonetheless, they are the standard by which I constantly measure myself.

Paul Robeson's influence on my life has helped me in my dealings with whites. There has been such bitterness within me over the condition of black people in this country that for a time I actually believed that all whites were my enemies. Today I feel that the crux of the problem lies in white racism and exploitation. Robeson allowed me to see beyond the injustices, to the fact that there are also whites who see me as a human being.

Robeson revealed to me that the cultures of humanity have been so interwoven that none can claim exclusivity. I still am a foe of racism—white racism. I do not recognize black racism as being a reality in this country.

Robeson helped me to understand the broad sweep of humanity extending through eternity and also taught me that I had the responsibility to make an explicit contribution to the struggles of our people. It is not enough to be good at a craft. One must use that craft as a weapon against the enemies of one's people.

CHAPTER 10

The most rewarding dimension of my enlightened life is producing documentaries. *Like It Is* uses a magazine format whereby each week several subjects are presented. Some programs consist of a fifteen-minute film, a half-hour studio discussion, and a commentary. Other programs can be devoted to one subject, often using a panel discussion or a film interview, such as the show with Jamaican Prime Minister Michael Manley. We are able to produce three or four major documentaries each year in this fashion.

WABC-TV has been subjected to pressure from several corners of the black community over the caliber of the network's programming. *Like It Is* was a few years old then but was nonetheless not in prime time. The critics pointed out that WABC-TV had yet to air prime-time programming (Monday through Friday from 7:00 P.M. to 11:00 P.M., Eastern time) that had been wholly produced by blacks. As a result, I was assigned to do a prime-time program about black music.

The title of the show was "Jazz—the American Art Form." I contacted Dizzy Gillespie, and we talked in his north-Jersey home about doing a documentary on the subject of which he was a primary exponent. It became clear that the hour alloted to the show would not be nearly enough time to make even a dent in the story of jazz. Dizzy told me that the history of jazz was most important and that we should emphatically state that the branches of the broad spectrum of American music—jazz, pop, rock, gospel, swing, rag, bop, and blues—all stemmed from a common African root.

Gillespie felt that his participation in the documentary would have to be put into perspective. He didn't want it to seem that trumpet playing began and ended with him. He was dismayed that blacks in the United States derided blacks in the Caribbean and Latin America, and vice versa. He wanted to interweave throughout the documentary the message that we all have the same origins. "We may have come to this hemisphere in different ships, but we are all in the same boat."

Gillespie explained that his style of playing was compatible with the music played in New Orleans and that he had jammed with many Dixieland groups. He had also played with calypso bands without problems of communication. I agreed that all these statements should be made.

I mapped out the documentary and shooting schedule and did several interviews with Dizzy. We flew to New Orleans to film him playing with a Dixieland band in a club.

After an overnight stay, we caught a flight to Jamaica, where Gillespie was to sit in with a calypso band in Kingston. When we touched down at Manley airport in Kingston, I experienced some personal trauma. It was my first trip to the land of my parents, who were both dead. They had left me with many rich things, among which was an impression of Jamaica as a paradise beyond belief. This lifelong concept was about to be tested.

We were on the island for a whirlwind two days, up half the night filming Dizzy with the band at the Sheraton Hotel. After the jazz session, we were all tired and decided to swim in the hotel pool. There were a number of lovely women lounging around the pool, and when Dizzy saw this, he sucked in his paunch and strode magnificently across the pool area, smiling charmingly at them. As all eyes followed him, Dizzy decided to extend himself. Not content to dive into the water from the pool's edge, he climbed on the high diving board. None of us even knew whether Dizzy could dive, but no one wanted to call out to him and break the spell he was weaving.

The jazz master sauntered to the edge of the board, belly held in, making his chest puff out like a rooster's, and bounced several times on the board before making a high arch and disappearing into the water.

I was the only one who saw that as he made the dive, Gillespie hit his shin on the edge of the board. I heard him whimper a second before he hit the water, but when he came to the surface, he was smiling broadly and got a round of applause from the admiring females. No one noticed the bruise on his leg. Dizzy Gillespie, world legend, exited the pool area and went into the men's room. I followed to see if he was really all right. The most heart-rending sobs met my ears, as Dizzy sat, doubled over, tenderly massaging his bruised shin.

Aside from these high jinks, we had a productive and successful stay in Jamaica. I took the camera crew into the mountains to shoot footage of the Jamaican topography. At this point, I fell in love with the island. Now I understood the special quality of life my parents had spoken of.

The beauty of the island is enhanced by its people, a considerate and warm community. No one is addressed in Jamaica without a polite greeting first, saying, "Good morning," or "Good afternoon." The children won my heart in their school uniforms, eyes bright and faces shining. The marketplaces buzz with conversation, and one is instantly drawn into the native dialogue. No one purchases anything at the quoted price—to do so would be to insult the seller. Everyone learns to haggle—to walk away in mock indignation and return, setting an equitable price, whereupon smiles are exchanged with the transaction. The fruit market is a fragrant and colorful display of tropical produce—star apples, naseberries, mangoes (more than twenty varieties), jack fruit, and coconuts. The odors and sweet juices make one drunk with pleasure.

The sun is hot, yet never overwhelming, because there is almost always a breeze gently blowing, expecially in the mountains. That trip was the beginning of a love affair with Jamaica that will never end for me. Jamaica is beautiful and also the cradle of my inheritance.

I also admire the efforts by the government to bring about a more equitable distribution of wealth. I bought land in the tiny town where my father was born, and the property looks out over the ocean waters where he was baptized.

Upon our return to New York, loaded down the precious film for the jazz documentary, I realized that my work was just beginning. I had to research the entire history and development of the music and dig through the musty film archives for clips of the jazz legends I wanted to include.

Within the treasure trove, I found clips of Billie Holiday, Lester Young, a youthful Louis Armstrong, an early clip of Duke Ellington, Nat King Cole, Count Basie, George Gershwin, Charlie Parker, Art Tatum, and other great names in jazz. I also interviewed Eubie Blake, who gave me a fascinating account of how two black men, Willie ("the Lion") Smith and Lucky Roberts, taught Gershwin to play the style of music he became famous for.

Eubie also clarified who the real "King of Jazz" was—James Reese Europe, who gave the first black concert at Carnegie Hall with an orchestra of more than a hundred pieces.

The result of my exciting acquaintance with jazz went on the air at Channel 7 in a prime-time slot. I recently took another look at that show, and it still has value and relevance. Much of its significance rests in the fact that it was the first prime-time documentary, produced by a black, that WABC-TV ever aired.

The documentary on Malcolm X was produced in 1969 and was aired on *Like It Is* in a non-prime-time slot.

Although I had worked long hours with a film editor and wrote, narrated, and researched the Malcolm X show, when we recorded the documentary on videotape, I noticed that Charles Hobson, who had come to *Like It Is* from the producer pool of WNET's *Black Journal*, was listed as the producer. When I confronted him about it, he said he was sorry. "It was an oversight," he said. "It will be corrected." That oversight has never been corrected.

The documentary was the first ever produced on Malcolm. It received critical acclaim. The show was put into distribution and sold to schools and colleges across the nation and the world. The distributor was obligated to pay the producer, who was listed as Charles Hobson. Hobson has reportedly received money from the distributor, Grove Press, for a documentary he didn't produce. I have never received a check from Hobson or from Grove Press.

However, things often have a way of working out. In 1976 I did a more extensive documentary on Malcolm X, entitled *El Haij Malik El Shabazz.* This program was awarded an Emmy by the Academy of Television Arts and Sciences in 1976 as outstanding documentary. It was put into distribution by McGraw-Hill and goes to schools and colleges throughout the United States.

Several other documentaries of mine have followed the same path. Those on Adam Clayton Powell, Martin Luther King, Paul Robeson, and the student role in the civil rights movement of the 1960s are all now in distribution.

103

Assembling a documentary is difficult work. The research comes first. Then the facts are assembled and a point of view is selected for the piece. It is important to check out the widest possible variety of sources, because facts are often reported inconsistently. One historian's viewpoint will vary from another's, depending on the biases of the individuals. It has been said that history is what any two people decide has happened in the past.

After the research is complete, the archives are raided to locate the film to support the facts. It is interesting to note that few file cards dated before 1950 list blacks as such. The now-unfashionable terms *Negro* or *colored* were used before then. Some of the descriptions on the file cards refer to us as "darkies" and even "coons." Film on Harlem and its inhabitants is listed under the heading *Ghetto*.

In seeking footage on Marcus Garvey, I found there was only a thirty-second bit of the famous clip of the man seated in an open car during a UNIA parade on Lenox Avenue. Such shortages of film on important black figures and events force the producer to bring all his or her creativity into play to make a well-rounded program. Alternatives available for use to illustrate a subject are artists' drawings, for instance. I myself have done sketches and used them in the documentary on Malcolm X to cover his early days as a slickster in Roxbury, Massachusetts. One learns to use the technique of filming still photographs, zooming in and out of the shot to add impact. There are many still shots available of early black Americans like Garvey, and with the audience in mind and a moderate hand, this way of portraying a subject can be effective.

Another source of additional material is newsreels. An emotionally moving shot of Depression-era soup lines in the 1930s can add force to accompanying narration, such as: "While Marcus Garvey was building his UNIA movement, the great Depression had millions of Americans in desperate straits."

104

Animation is another possibility, but it is enormously expensive to produce. The host or narrator of the show may also appear at an appropriate locale to describe events that took place there, although I prefer to stick to the subject and not focus on the reporter so much.

When the research is done and the film problem solved, a script can be written. My guiding rule in writing comes from my background as a newsman—brevity, first and last. No matter how beautifully I may have written copy, I go over it again and again to pare it down to the bone.

I have learned that material needs to run in varying time lengths, because American audiences have been increasingly programmed to viewing tastes that will not tolerate an overlong documentary. I have started doing "mini-docs" about people and events in black history, with young audiences specifically in mind. *Like It Is* has done such short shows as "Charlie Parker," "Ragtime Music," "Erroll Garner," "Booker T. Washington," "George Washington Carver," and "The Role of Black Women Liberators." These programs run from five to fifteen minutes in length and are highly visual and to the point.

We have produced several "essays," a form of documentary, with subjects like "Hair Corn-Rowing" and "Our Many Ways of Loving." We also produced a three-part miniseries called *From Superman to Man,* based on the work of the black historian J. A. Rogers, which concerned a hypothetical confrontation between a white southern senator and a black railroad porter over the issue of equality of the races. The senator takes the offensive early in the argument but is very quietly cut down to size by the porter, who is armed with facts. In winning his points, the porter tells about black achievements and contributions.

The last of my recent mini-docs is a six-part series aired on *Like It Is* called *Africa's Gifts to the World,* with each segment running about ten minutes. The visuals are slides supplied by the noted

105

artist Don Miller. Historian John Henrik Clarke was the consultant for the program. Each segment dealt with a specific contribution that Africa has made to the world family in art, metallurgy, architecture, or agriculture, or portrayed other aspects of African history, such as slavery and Timbuktu.

Documentaries are extremely important as a modern counterpart of the textbook. Because today's young generation is vastly more oriented to media than their parents were, the film documentary is a conduit of information to youth. Many schools are using film documentaries in the classroom. Unfortunately, fewer than a handful of these films have been assembled by black filmmakers.

I have had tremendous reaction from students who have seen my documentaries. The impact of seeing a historic event take place has far more effect for many than merely reading about it.

As I lobby for support of the documentary, I am aware of the high cost of producing them. Budgets often start at two thousand dollars per aired minute and sometimes much more. But in view of the importance of the material, I think it is worth the expense. Networks spend large sums on made-for-television feature films, and they make a profit. They are replayed and sometimes are shown in theaters nationally and internationally. The same could apply to the documentary. A crackling good documentary costs ten percent of what a made-for-television feature does. If well promoted, it can make money for the producing station.

I have already cited my feelings about the value of feature films on Doctor Martin Luther King and the Jewish holocaust versus documentary films on the same subject. Malcolm X has been portrayed in several "docu-dramas," but there isn't an actor alive who can successfully project the power and awesome charisma that were Malcolm's.

In order to make documentaries more attractive, several producers have engaged the services of well-known actors. Orson

Wells has narrated a few of these—most notably a documentary on the treasure of Tutankhamen. Sir Lawrence Olivier has narrated a series on World War II. The dashing Gregory Peck was hired to narrate ABC's four-hour documentary on Africa, which aired in the late 1960s.

The presence of media personalities adds luster to a documentary. Although they may know little about the content of the film, stars can attract unusual audience interest. Bill Cosby played this kind of role as host narrator of the CBS series on black images in film. Cosby's unusual ability to relate to audiences of all races proved a valuable instrument. Many who would automatically turn away from a documentary on such an issue stayed tuned because of Cosby's participation.

Alistair Cooke is enormously popular with media audiences, even though he is neither a movie star nor a documentary-film maker. He has a good on-camera presence, and his quiet dignity, coupled with an English accent, lends a ring of authority to the documentaries, some of which were rather badly slanted, such as the series he did on America. Mr. Cooke strolled through wheat fields and museums and rolled out the script on the beginning of this nation. It was obvious that no native Americans or blacks had any part in writing the script. On the merits of effectiveness alone, however, the work was well done. Significantly large audiences saw the series and were influenced and informed by it, and that is what media are about.

My point is that the documentary is a critically important device for informing and shaping minds that have grown flabby through watching entertainment-only television programming. Those who have the clout to change this situation should be asked why they do not air more documentary films.

The documentary remains the central issue of my professional career. It certainly is the most rewarding thing I do for television. I think the possibilities of expanding the documentary in scope

107

and style are limitless. It remains a powerful weapon to change false values, correct historical error, and cure the poison of prejudice in the minds of black and white Americans.

I hope that many more blacks enter all aspects of the documentary field.

CHAPTER **11**

World War I was fought by blacks as well as whites, and the young uniformed men marched off to be killed and maimed. Blacks fought in segregated units. When they returned from foreign lands, many veterans looked for some reward from this nation for the great sacrifices they had made. For black veterans, these hopes were dashed by the realities of racist America.

Open conflicts over jobs, between black and white veterans, escalated into full-scale riots. The Red Summer was a tragic example. Out of a deep disappointment and resentment at America's failure to be just, many blacks were drawn into a movement that had started in 1911 and was rapidly growing under the organizational name of the Universal Negro Improvement Association.

Marcus Garvey, a young labor activist from Jamaica was the leader. His thesis was that since the United States could not do right by the black race, the black race must find ways of doing for itself. Garvey stated that although we as a people were confined to these national boundaries, it would be wise for us to erect our own institutions.

Black-owned and -operated factories were set up in the Harlems of America. Garvey even designed black dolls, so that black children could have a better sense of identity than they got from blond and blue-eyed dolls.

The ultimate agenda of Garvey's organization was a vision of American blacks returning to Africa. He raised money to buy steamships to send millions of people to the continent from which their ancestors had been kidnapped.

The idea was shocking then and now. It was impossible for whites to think that black people would be ungrateful and want to leave this good hemisphere with all the wonderful things we enjoyed here. Garvey's idea triggered a deep feeling that had always lived in the marrow of our bones. The media and leadership of this country were shocked to discover that Garvey's back-to-Africa movement attracted millions of black followers. America has to face the historical fact that Marcus Garvey's black movement was the largest ever mobilized in the United States, larger than even the civil rights movement and the Nation of Islam.

The Garvey theses were, "Africa is better than here," and "Black is beautiful." Garvey staged monumental parades, in the major black communities of this country, that gave our hearts a surging sense of pride. Garvey awakened our dignity with his command "Up, you mighty race!" He explained the glories of our African roots and filled black hearts and minds with the desire to return to the homeland. He instructed us that we must become more independent while waiting to return to Africa.

Garvey had an extensive organizational structure, with several echelons of officials and lieutenants. The organization owned many business enterprises and had a substantial treasury. They had a militia, with fabulous uniforms. There was even a corps of nurses. The movement was international—there were UNIA branches in many countries, including South Africa.

This overpowering sense of black identity was very threatening to many powerful people in this country. These same powerful people had begun to make serious business overtures in Africa, many sugared with lies to the natives about how well their brothers and sisters were being treated in America.

Something had to be done to destroy the movement and stop Garvey. J. Edgar Hoover was the new head of the Federal Bureau of Investigation, and he embarked on the same course of undermining and illegal subversion that would be repeated years later against Paul Robeson, Adam Clayton Powell, Jr., and the entire civil rights movement.

FBI documentation shows that Garvey was a key target. He was plagued by rumor, his organization was infiltrated, and his actions were observed. Several FBI attempts were made to defame his character. The Treasury Department set upon him; he was charged with "improprieties." Blacks were paid to infiltrate his ranks and seek out weak spots to be attacked. Garvey was tried and convicted of tax irregularities and was deported.

It seemed that the government wanted to assure that he was completely removed from his followers. Garvey lived out the rest of his days in exile in England and Jamaica. The hopes of millions of blacks were crushed. Garvey's Black Star Line was eliminated. With Garvey out of the way, the movement floundered and died.

The destruction of Garvey's crusade dealt a serious blow to the positive sense of self among blacks in America. The hidden message was that we would never be able to stand up against the "American way of life." The only alternative was to accept things, work hard, and strive to become a part of the system—even if only a second-class part. Many blacks resigned themselves to low-echelon government jobs, domestic work, or running elevators.

Conversation about black pride disappeared, and the beautiful black dolls were no longer available. Even for the millions of blacks who had not joined Garvey's movement, it was a loss because they had secretly felt pride at Garvey and were discouraged when he was removed.

When *Amos 'n' Andy* hit the airwaves, the climate was ripe. We had been cheering Garvey's magnificent Universal Negro Improvement Association, and then returned to negativism, laughing along with whites at two black buffoons.

Eubie Blake, a beautiful ninety-five-year-old youngster, says, "Do you know the story of Paul Revere? Most everybody knows that story. But do you know the name of the horse that Paul Revere rode? Nobody knows the name of his horse. You know why? Because the horse didn't write the story!"

I love to hear Eubie tell that joke. Every time he runs it off, I laugh as hard as I did the first time, even though it really isn't funny.

In fact, the point Blake is making is a tragic one, if applied to the story of people of African descent in this country.

The black experience has been detailed to excess by nonblacks. Therefore, most people do not know our names—the names of significant people of my race who have made contributions for which we are all richer.

Amos 'n' Andy were two radio characters born in the minds of the white radio actors Charles Correll and Freeman Gosden. This comedy team made an indelible impression on Americans, an impression that survives to this day, although the program was one of the worst expressions of racism to pollute the airwaves.

Amos 'n' Andy was first broadcast in the earliest days of radio. Until that time, radio broadcasting was a tentative business. Stations were few and owned largely by individuals, not corporations or conglomerates. The commercial possibilities were considered small; radio was more of an electronic exercise and adventure than an investment.

Radio station owners suddenly saw that thousands of Americans were turning to radio for entertainment. Businessmen saw this too and decided to advertise their products experimentally on the air. The advertising produced sales, and radio as big business

112

was born. Commercials initially ran for varying lengths of time. It was many years before commercial time became structured, with rates based on the length of the piece and the time of day it was broadcast.

Announcers and commentators became known in every household. They covered parades, inaugurations, wars, riots, conventions, and baseball games. Eventually, the business of radio became so profitable that broadcasters built studios where they could create their own entertainment. Dramatizations and even concert performances were staged especially for radio. Singers, actors, and comedians were approached by radio-station owners to do performances on the air.

Not only was it the golden opportunity for artists to make money, but it also gave them a chance to get off the road and return to a normal family life.

Al Jolson, Paul Whiteman, Fred Allen, Jack Benny, and hundreds of other performers jumped on the radio bandwagon and off the vaudeville circuit. These performers soon became regularly identified with specific radio programs and serials.

The supporting businesses (now known as sponsors) were just as eager as the performers to mine the possibilities of the infant radio industry. Mr. and Mrs. America and all the ships at sea were soon addicted to an avalanche of scheduled radio fare. The key in-gredients were: star performers, a program name, a format, and a sponsor. Eventually sponsors became more aggressive. Instead of simply buying air time on programs that had been conceived by the stations, they assembled their own and went into the produc-tion end of radio. These programs were delivered to the radio stations complete and ready for broadcast with commercials sand-wiched in. The sponsors paid a fee to the station for the air time.

President Herbert Hoover was such a devout radio fan that he left strict orders that he not be disturbed while *Amos 'n' Andy* was on. The president of the United States deferred affairs of state for fifteen minutes in order to laugh as he listened to the fictitious drama about black people. Hoover was known for his apathetic attitude toward blacks and native Americans, which certainly didn't dilute his love for the exploitative show.

The president personally invited Freeman Gosden and Charles Correll to the White House, where the actors were asked to renact favorite episodes of the program. Coolidge had memorized many of the sequences, and he joined in with the performers as they delivered their routines in person. The enthusiasm the president of the United States exhibited for *Amos 'n' Andy* served as a seal of approval and guaranteed even larger American audiences for the racially biased material.

Amos 'n' Andy made millions of dollars for Lever Brothers. The theme—a whistled tune—backed the commercial for Rinso soap and was heard across America as audiences held their sides aching from laughter at the cruel depiction of blacks. Today *Amos 'n' Andy* is synonymous with Uncle Tom and other negative racial symbols.

Not only whites were victimized by this prejudicial programming; even blacks were taken in. My family listened and laughed at the comedy team. It was one of the few opportunities for us to feed anything black-oriented to our image-hungry minds.

America was a lynch-spirited, segregated society where the notion of blacks living outside ghetto communities like Harlem was unthinkable. We had no positive image from the mass media, so we settled for far less. We were not told about anything black in public schools. In the movies, no blacks were shown except an occasional Stepin Fetchit. There were no blacks in major-league baseball. When *Amos 'n' Andy* reached the ears of black people, most failed to consider the slap against their race. It was then enough to merely receive attention of any sort.

The National Association for the Advancement of Colored People (NAACP) eventually issued a strong denunciation of the radio program as demeaning to the black race, but few blacks learned of this condemnation because it was ignored by mass media and radio news.

Conditions in America were hardly geared towards the progress of blacks as an equal segment of the total population. The twentieth century was not yet thirty years old. Blacks still bore the physical and mental scars of one of history's most brutal and extreme forms of oppression. The years of oppressive treatment had stifled most open rebellion. Blacks fortunate enough to get some degree of education had seen what was done to people like Denmark Vesey and Nat Turner in past centuries. For some blacks in America, a hope welled that there would come a day when better conditions for their people would exist.

Marcus Garvey's countenance was proud and militant. He wore a plumed helmet and rode in an open carriage in the extraordinary parades. Amos wore a smirk on his lips, a leer in his eyes, and a bowler derby, and he drove a taxi.

Garvey spoke of African kings and dynasties and of controlling our black destiny and politics. Amos talked of dodging the credit man and the bill collector and never about politics.

As bad as the early days of radio were for black self-image, they were mild compared to what we are confronted with today. Television reaches far more people than early radio did, and when one views program fare, *Amos 'n' Andy* lives on.

The program *Sanford and Son* is the same denigrating format. Fred Sanford is the reincarnation of Amos, displaying the same indolence and the same lack of respect for honest work and black women. The program also portrays the same preoccupation with getting something for nothing.

Today's television offerings replay the Garvey scenario. The civil rights movement of the 1960s produced another groundswell of black resistance to racism, and its leaders have been made ineffectual or have been eliminated. Malcolm X, Doctor King,

115

Elijah Muhammad, and Medgar Evers are all gone. These leaders of the civil rights movement were victims of a government conspiracy in the same way that Garvey was, and the strategy architect was the same John Edgar Hoover.

Black people must have more participation in the control of the television diet consumed by the American public. Otherwise, we will all be doomed to repeating the same errors and falling victim to the same misconceptions of the past. Blacks must produce films and TV programs. Producers must not be afraid to create material that is informative and positive.

Our youngsters need to be taught the facts about the black struggle and those who waged it. It is fine to know the name of Paul Revere, as Eubie Blake says, but we must also know the name of the horse, and that story must come straight from the horse's mouth.

CHAPTER **12**

I have developed a warm friendship with Paul Robeson, Jr., through the years since I produced a documentary on the life of his father. In researching the project, I visited the principal repository of information on Robeson—the Paul Robeson Archives, which were put together five or six years before Robeson's death.

Eventually I met Paul, Jr., and told him of my research needs. My head was filled with misinformation about his father, and we circled each other like prizefighters. I was then unable to produce the piece because of limitations at *Like It Is*, and this situation didn't exactly endear me to Paul, Jr.

In 1975, when I became the producer of *Like It Is*, I renewed my quest for a show on Robeson. I had a larger budget to work with and a production team under my direction.

Paul, Jr., slowly began to cooperate, giving me material from the archives to study. I always returned with new questions and arguments, and Paul would patiently release more information and answer my needs. We began to talk informally and soon found ourselves in deep conversations.

The archive documents backed up the awesome things Paul, Jr., told me about his father. I scoured pounds of newspaper clippings and read through the writings of Paul Robeson, Sr., who was then alive but suffering from arteriosclerosis and other medical complications that had forced him into permanent retirement in Philadelphia. He lived there, in a frame house, with his sister, Marion. No one was able to see him except a few life-long friends and his family.

Paul, Jr., had assembled a monumental storehouse of information about his father. Included was documentation of how Robeson had been vilified by many agencies of the federal government, as well as the media. I saw copies of memorandums from the files of the FBI and read newspaper stories announcing that NBC radio had banned Robeson from an appearance on a program hosted by Eleanor Roosevelt. The National Broadcasting Company had decided that Robeson's political views were intolerable and that he was never to be allowed on the network.

The archives collection has now been donated to Howard University. My friendship with Paul, Jr., is still strong and growing. We look forward to many future collaborations, including a book that will document the extensive effort that the FBI made to destroy Paul Robeson on every level.

Several documents, released by the Bureau under the Freedom of Information Act, reveal a number of horrendous plots against the man. It is our duty to bring this information to the public and make people aware of the insidious power of such agencies.

Adam Clayton Powell, Jr., was another prominent black figure who attracted my professional attention. Although I never established a friendship with the man, I did meet him several times and interviewed him at the Abyssinian Baptist Church. He was an impressive man—tall, brilliant, angry, and in possession of a quick sense of humor.

The clouds had begun to gather over the final chapter of his congressional career when I met him. He was beset by the pressures of the case of Esther James, a woman who sued him because he had publicly called her a bagwoman for the police in

Harlem. Powell felt that it was common knowledge that James was a bagwoman, but proving it was something else. Powell held repeated press conferences in his church concerning the James case, and that is where I first saw him in person.

Powell laced his answers to reporters with quips and jokes. Congress was concurrently rising up in indignation over Powell's involvement in the "scandalous" affair, and they were out to punish him for alleged misdeeds.

Powell waved aside the charges by stating that he had done nothing as a congressman that others hadn't already done. He said that if he was wrong, the entire congressional body was wrong. He asked repeatedly why he was being singled out. Was it because he had acquired too much power and influence as chairman of the Education and Labor Committee in Congress? Powell had been in Congress for more than twenty years, and he had a certain control over almost half of the domestic budget of the nation.

He warned that if pushed too far by his colleagues in Congress, he would make public all he knew about them, and he declared that he knew plenty. I asked Powell if I could have a private word with him after the news conference and then explained who I was and the nature of my work. I asked him to go before my camera and relate the wrongdoings of his congressional colleagues. He said that he would consider the offer and get back to me, but he never did.

I tried to contact him again several times, to no avail. I saw him at subsequent news conferences, and I always pressed my offer. One day I caught up with him and succeeded in getting him before my camera after he had been expelled from congress and had written a book titled *Adam by Adam*.

Powell had flown from his Bimini home, where he was in retirement, to make public appearances and give interviews to promote his book. The publicists for the book approached me on the day he had come to ABC to appear on another show and

119

asked if I wanted to interview the ex-congressman. I gathered up a film crew and as much unexposed film stock as I could find.

Powell talked with me for more than an hour and gave a fascinating account of his life. Years later, it served as the backbone of my documentary on him. I asked about corruption on Capitol Hill, and he corroborated the existence of rampant criminal activities in Congress, but he would not name names. I later asked his wife, Hazel Scott, why Powell avoided the questions he knew the answers to, and she explained that Adam felt it would have been too damaging to the Congress and to the country to reveal the facts. In spite of what had been done to the man, he was always concerned about protecting the system that had crucified him.

I later saw Powell on the day he lost the election to Charles Rangel, marking the end of his brilliant and turbulent career. I was in Harlem seeking footage of voter activity at the polls, and I saw him at the corner of 135th Street and Seventh Avenue. (The Harlem part of Seventh Avenue would later be named Adam Clayton Powell, Jr., Boulevard.) He was about to be interviewed by Gene Simpson, a black colleague of mine from WCBS-TV. I asked Powell if he would give me an interview, and he said, "Sure."

I stood nearby while Simpson did his interview, anxious to hear his line of questioning. As the other newsman's cameraman started to roll his film, a police prowl car passed and one of the officers called out to Powell. Powell felt no love for the police after they had refused to support his accusation of Mrs. James, but he forced a smile to his lips and answered, "What say, baby?" As the prowl car moved away, he muttered, "You jive turkeys."

Powell quickly turned to Gene Simpson and said, "I hope your camera wasn't rolling on that." Simpson said that it had been but that the remark would never be aired. Later, Simpson called me, deeply distraught. The film had been delivered to the newsroom and edited by a writer who refused to obey Simpson's instructions about cutting out the remark Powell had made to the police. The film was shown with Powell in Harlem calling out a smirking greeting to unseen people and then muttering the deprecating afterword. The viewer, not knowing that Powell was addressing the police, would be led to assume that he was talking in such a hypocritical fashion to Harlemites.

Simpson felt that he had let Powell down. I advised him to call Powell immediately and tell him what had happened. Simpson wanted to go further. He had been having problems with WCBS, which felt the black newsman was "difficult" to work with, a familiar problem for blacks who work in white-owned firms.

I do not know the outcome. But viewers who saw the report on television that evening were badly misled about an already heavily maligned public figure. Simpson was eventually fired from WCBS-TV news, and he then countered by suing the company, charging discriminatory practices. The suit was filed with the New York City Human Rights Commission. I don't know if there is a connection between the two events.

I relate this incident to illustrate how stories can be distorted and perverted in the media. I don't know who the writer was who cut the Simpson interview with Powell, but it is fair to ask why that exchange with the police was shown, unexplained, especially since it was so far removed from the key story, the election.

I saw Powell once again, a few days after the election in which Rangel defeated him. Powell had organized a news conference to charge that there had been tampering with the tabulated votes. He called for a recount because he had been defeated by an extremely narrow margin.

Powell did not look good, but the old fires still burned within him. His work as a congressman puts him at the top of the list of legislators who worked for our people. I am sure that he did wrong—but when the entire package is examined, we must give

121

him credit. He played hard, but he worked hard too.

Many outstanding black leaders have come out of the church. Powell, King, Robeson, and Malcolm are all such figures. I first saw Martin Luther King in Harlem, when he delivered a powerful sermon at the Convent Avenue Baptist Church. He made an indelible impression on me at the time and later, at news conferences connected with the civil rights movement in the New York City area.

King was more subdued at news conferences than when in the pulpit. He spoke softly and slowly and selected his words carefully. His experiences with the media had taught him to be wary.

When he arrived in Newark, New Jersey, after the terrible 1967 upheavals, he was accorded a hero's welcome, with a motorcade and press coverage. King also held a news conference, which I covered for WABC-TV News. A number of questions were asked about candidates in the upcoming presidential election. Most of the questions concerned the Democrats, and at the end of the conference, I asked King why no mention of the Republican candidate, Richard Nixon, had been made. King said that "Brother" Nixon had absolutely no relevance to the concerns of the civil rights movement and its goals and that it would be a tragic setback to the black struggle if he were elected.

King's words were prophetic. After the conference, I shook his hand and mentioned a new phrase—"sock-it-to-it-iveness"—and said that the expression might be applied to many of his statements. He laughed.

I saw King again in the winter of 1967-68 at a Manhattan night spot called Hickory House. My wife and I had gone there to hear the Billy Taylor Trio. She pointed out King and his party on the other side of the room, but by that time, I was at serious odds with King's philosophy, which refused to allow blacks to defend themselves against attack. My feelings were so strong that I didn't talk to him that night.

Had I been more mature, I would have thanked him for all that he had done for our people. But those were angry and confused days for me. Many of us had vacillating opinions and ethics. The most enduring thoughts I have of King center on his strong moral will and that tremendous courage. He willingly laid his body on the line for justice. I continue to be touched and recharged when I think of his great honesty and strength of conviction.

CHAPTER 13

Television can change things. It is a powerful mind-molding machine, and it could make people concerned about their very real problems, instead of preoccupying them with the problems of fictitious families of the soap operas and situation comedies.

I am not saying that TV shouldn't be entertaining. Several years ago, a brilliant writer named Langston Hughes wrote a series of columns about a Harlemite who frequents a bar and engages in extended dialogues with the bartender. The two men discuss everything from the Harlem social scene to world politics. *Simple Speaks His Mind* was hilarious, yet thought provoking.

Why are television networks so timid in presenting such fine material? There is a long list of works by black writers that would make excellent fare for television audiences, whether overtly political works were included or not.

A dramatic film could be produced about the life of Josephine Baker and also of the actor Ira Aldrich. George Washington Carver has not yet been brought to life on the television screen.

Why not commission and air the work of black writers? Less than one tenth of one percent of the TV dramatic programs are written by blacks, and an even smaller percentage of programs aired on television are produced by blacks. Sidney Poitier is a tried and proven director and producer who has never been utilized in the television industry. Harry Belafonte is one of the most skilled and capable producers in the entertainment business, and yet he has been repeatedly ignored. Other valuable blacks are Vinette Carroll, Geoffrey Holder, and Douglas Turner Ward. Each of these people have won the highest recognition for their skills, yet has been passed over by an industry that is starved for new and exciting material.

The Negro Ensemble Company (NEC) is an outstanding example of how Broadway has come to capitalize on black talent. The Ensemble was founded in 1967 by Douglas Turner Ward, Robert Hooks (a former colleague on *Like It Is*), and Gerald Krone to provide a theatrical spawning ground for black talent.

It has operated from a building in New York's East Village since its inception and has developed a host of skillful playwrights and actors, as well as dancers, comedians, and singers. Many of the names have become familiar to the nation, such as Denise Nichols of *Room 222* TV fame. Several of the NEC's productions have done well enough to move to Broadway. Joseph A. Walker's *The River Niger* enjoyed a long run on the Great White Way and received high critical acclaim.

Dozens of theatrical companies in Harlem are turning out fascinating and imaginative productions, among them the Afro American Total Theater and the National Black Theatre, Inc. These creative blacks are being shunted aside by the incestuous clique of writers and producers who continually dish out the same stereotypes of the California jet-set world they themselves move in. The Los Angeles TV colony, its members' value system, and their way of life are based on keeping up with their own kind. There is little opportunity for the inclusion of fresh blood or of different people in their midst, unless, of course, the newcomers are exactly like them. These people go to the same parties and discos and pursue the same fashion trends and the same political

126

causes. I am not saying that what they are about is invalid; I merely suggest that there are other people, other values, backgrounds, and pursuits that are never given a shot at the world of television production.

The situation comedies are almost predictable in their plots and characterizations. Even when blacks are presented, they fall into the same value system as the white programs.

Researchers should explore the black communities of America for new TV material. The Schomburg Library on the corner of Harlem's Lenox Avenue and 135th Street, is a rich repository of plays—comedies and dramas—that will blow the American viewing mind. Film archives contain films that were produced by blacks, such as Oscar Michaux, and that feature black actors. There are a multitude of interesting ideas for TV material, including the story of how and why the existing black films were made.

Frank Silvera, Canada Lee, Frederick O'Neal, Rose Mc-Clendon, and countless others built their careers in a theatrical world that white theater has yet to acknowledge fully. Harry Belafonte told me in an interview of how he was launched as a performer through his involvement with the Theatre Guild in Harlem in the 1940s.

He related how he moved up from a stage hand in the company to a performer, and how he became friends with another young actor named Sidney Poitier, who eventually became Harry's understudy in one of the productions. As luck and providence would have it, the night that Harry couldn't make his appearance on stage was the opportunity for Poitier to impress several people who had come from downtown theater to search for a black actor. They hired Poitier, not knowing he was Belafonte's understudy. From there, Sidney went on to a movie career that still blooms.

Both Belafonte and Poitier have been unsuccessful in making

127

any major inroads in TV production. Harry has produced several TV entertainment specials but has had no ongoing response from TV executives on his ideas for producing other, more serious material. Poitier has met with the same frustrations.

Lorraine Hansberry wrote a television play that was never aired by the TV stations that paid for it because it was deemed "too provocative." Richard Wright, John Oliver Killens, James Baldwin, and Maya Angelou are all black writers who could enrich us if their works were seen on TV.

Television hasn't reached its potential in airing music, either. The Saturday-night "specials" feature ridiculous musical acts and rarely showcase genuine artists, such as Sarah Vaughan, Don Shirley, Dizzy Gillespie or Phineas Newborn. Are we not all the poorer for this neglect? If you think John Lennon can play the guitar, have you ever heard and watched Kenny Burrell? Why is Liberace a household name, when Art Tatum remains relatively unknown to this day? (And although Tatum's name is better known today than it once was, when this great jazz artist died, he had barely a hundred dollars in his possession.)

NBC can be commended for heavily financing a special show on Artur Rubinstein. I am certain that it was produced at a revenue loss, but what a splendid document we now have of a great artist. CBS can be saluted for producing the memorable *Dial M for Music* special aired some twenty years ago, which featured Thelonious Monk, Count Basie, Billie Holiday, Lester Young, Ben Webster, Harry Edison, and Jimmy Rushing. It stands as one of television's best presentations of America's only complete and original art form.

These great artists were brought into the CBS studios and invited to play without reimbursement, so the show was not costly. The host, John Crosby, dubbed in the introductions, and the film was edited into a program. Unfortunately, there have been few similar shows during the two following decades. The result is that the current young generation worships mediocrity.

These children, not being exposed to true artistic greatness, have fallen for the musical pap that has been fed them. Small wonder that today's young musicians believe that the way to succeed as a performer is to wear an open shirt and tight pants and boast a 45-foot-tall amplifier!

My favorite rock group, though, remains the Rolling Stones, for their prejudiced recording "Some Girls." This song explicitly verbalizes an obscene characterization of black women as being immoral.

> *White girls, they're pretty funny.*
> *Sometimes they drive you mad.*
> *Black girls, they just want to f—— all night.*
> *I just don't have that much jam.*

The FCC's failure to react to this pus being broadcast on the radio is infuriating. There was an outcry against this record in the black community, and the head of the recording company that released the album issued a public apology. He stated that the album would be removed from the shelves of the record stores, but that never happened. When Mick Jagger was approached and told of the criticisms of his tune, he reportedly replied, "If they can't take a joke, f—— 'em."

Television has not produced any editorials about the evil tune—except for *Like It Is*. The Stones continue to receive heavy airtime exposure, even though it angers blacks who are injured by the implications. Meanwhile, serious black artists get little, if any, air exposure at all. Television *can* do better.

Like It Is has been kept on the air by WABC-TV for a decade, even though many of our programs have expressed views that caused many people to get uptight. I would be more than a hypocrite if I didn't express my gratitude to management for this. At the same time, my criticisms of TV will continue until there is

129

an end to racism on the nation's television screens.

My old colleague, Bill McCreary, hosts *Black News* on WNEW-TV, an independent station owned by Westinghouse. That program has given those who watch Channel 5 their only perspective of news events through a black editorial lens. The program is essentially a newscast, presenting a digest of the news stories of the preceding week that concern Third World issues. They use footage and excerpts of materials aired in the previous week's nightly broadcasts.

Bill McCreary plays a valuable role, since he lends his expertise as a reporter in assembling the program. The result is a unique flavor in *Black News* that separates it from other black-oriented programs.

WCBS-TV has been straddling the fence. The station hasn't aired a specifically black-oriented program for years. They broadcast a weekly program called *Channel 2 The People*, but it lacks a consistent premise.

Vic Miles, the anchorman for one of the weeknight newscasts, has been the recent host of this show. Miles has the journalistic experience, but it appears that he is able to spend very little time, if any, preparing or being involved with the program. It may be that the news department doesn't give him enough time off from his other news duties.

WOR-TV has one black program, as does WPIX-TV. It is good that they exist, but I am most unhappy that they don't receive the attention and push that white shows do. Alma John is the elder stateswoman of the TV talk shows on black issues. She is a dear, sweet person who has worked hard to offer a sustained contribution to our cause as a people. The management of the station that airs the program she has hosted, *Black Pride*, has failed to promote the show. In fact, they have practically ignored her.

WNET is an educational station and thus is free from the shackles of commercialism; yet it has a bleak record on offering black-oriented programs. Today, they don't air a single regularly scheduled black-controlled program out of their New York-New Jersey-Connecticut broadcast area. WNET does air a black-produced program that comes out of Philadelphia, called *Black Perspectives on the News*, which is broadcast nationally. WNET is reputedly a liberal station, but it is anything but that. My personal opinion is that WNET is the most biased of the TV stations in the New York metropolitan area. It has no black producers. Ellis Haslip did once produce a dramatic series called *Watch Your Mouth*, but that program was quickly dropped.

WNET doesn't broadcast in Newark, the city in which it is licensed to operate by the Federal Communications Commission. All its offices and studios are in Manhattan. The station receives grants from the state of New York for its programs. Its directors have rendered themselves eligible for this funding through cleverly incorporating themselves in New York State in order to receive hundreds of thousands of dollars in grants annually from the New York State Council on the Arts. I was a panel member of the Council and reviewed their grant proposals.

WNET has dealt an injury to its audience in not producing black programming and in having its operations in Manhattan, rather than Newark (which is mostly black). The number of ancillary jobs surrounding a TV station are thus denied to Newark and its residents. The city could profit from the technical, financial, service-operations, shopping, restaurants, entertainment, hotel, and other businesses generated by WNET operating from its environs.

Broadcasters also tend to focus on their immediate turf, which explains why so little news and coverage of Newark, Jersey City, and other towns in that district is covered on WNET. This is a slap against the audiences and citizens who would benefit from proper programming at this station.

CHAPTER 14

In 1959, the United States government staged a gargantuan exhibition, similar to a World's Fair, in Sokolniki Park, Moscow. The purpose of the exhibit was to present an impressive array of Americana for Soviet citizens to see and, it was hoped, eat their hearts out at what they were missing. It was a sprawling show, with innumerable pavilions covering art, automobiles, domestic living, movies, fashion, and other areas. Several major United States corporations took part in the displays, and each of the pavilions put on several shows per day for the huge crowds of Muscovites. I was chosen to be part of the performing group in the fashion pavilion. It was enormous fun, and the occasion became the focal point for my wedding.

At the time I was selected to go to the Soviet Union, I had been working for Union Carbide and had a bachelor apartment in Harlem. I had been seriously involved in the profound and demanding occupation of woman chasing when I met my future wife, Jean. I immediately began seeing less of the other women I had been running with, and within three months, Jean and I discussed spending our future together.

I did the whole number, including going through the excruciating formality of asking Jean's parents for her hand in

133

marriage. Soon after our engagement, my friend Don Ramsay, a male model, called to ask if I was interested in being his alternate for the Soviet fashion show.

I had met Don through my excursions into the world of modeling. From time to time I would take an extended lunch hour from my Union Carbide job and pick up extra money posing for ads. Since I am six feet, five inches tall, I was restricted from doing regular modeling, and there were precious few jobs for black male models in any event. Don's offer was highly appealing, and I agreed.

Several days later I was summoned to the Fashion Institute of Technology, where a panel reviewed my appearance. I was asked to walk, smile, and talk extemporaneously, after which I was selected in place of Don Ramsay, although I never discovered why.

Since I'd be making the trip, I would have to alter plans for my wedding, which had been scheduled to take place at the same time as the ten-week trip to the U.S.S.R. Jean never suggested that I not go, although she was obviously disappointed, as were our families.

The next weeks were busy with meetings and rehearsals for the participants in the show. Many of the group of twenty were not professional models. They included an entire family, several teenagers, and a few male and female models. The organizers of the fashion exhibit wanted to present to the Soviets a believable representation of American citizens.

The publicity department asked me for a biography, which contained the information that I was engaged to be married. I was the only black male in the group and had been chosen along with Jackie Clay, a black woman. Another black was needed, and I was asked if my fiancee would agree to be interviewed for the show. Jean wowed the panel and was accepted on the spot.

We departed Idlewilde (now Kennedy) Airport and stopped

first at Shannon Airport in Ireland. From there, we continued on to Finland and then to the Soviet Union.

We had all taken a cram course in Russian, but it barely equipped us to maneuver in public. We never felt uncomfortable, though, despite our inability to communicate. The Soviets were very warm and kind to us. Crowds followed us everywhere, and Jean and I were of particular interest because there are few blacks in Russia.

Each member of the exhibit team was given a salary and a living allowance, and we all roomed in the same Moscow hotels, the Ostanksinkaya and the Leningradskaya.

Moscow is a magnificent city. The avenues dwarf those in this country, seeming to be at least four times as wide. The city is filled with museums and statues, many of them glorifying Soviet heroes.

We often got around town with public transportation, and I can vouch for the Soviet subway system, which puts New York's transit system to shame. The Moscow underground has wonderful escalators that carry passengers deep below the surface, where the subway platforms are cavernous and clean. The trains are lovely—sleek, fast, and silent. The only discomfort I suffered in riding the subways was being ogled by the people. When I entered a car, word quickly spread throughout the train, and people would crowd around me and stare. Perhaps it was training for the public career that was ahead of me.

The fashion pavilion put on three or four performances each day. Jean and I enacted our carefully rehearsed routines, which had us wearing costumes in a variety of situations created by the director-choreographer Joe Layton. We performed on a raised platform shaped like a crescent. The stage entrance to the platform was in the crescent's center, and the platform and surrounding area were sheltered by a pale green plastic canopy, to protect us from the elements. The program was a huge success, although

135

inevitably, there were some political snags to be untangled.

Several top designer houses in America had entered their clothes in our show. Objections were raised about one scene in which Jean and I were supposedly married and our bogus attendants were white. Eventually, the marriage sequence was dropped from the performance. That was a shame, because Jean had been fitted with an exquisite wedding gown and she looked stunning during rehearsals.

What seems ironic was that the United States staged an exhibit to put its best foot forward in the U.S.S.R., and blacks were deliberately included to prevent the Soviets from labeling the effort phony and racist. Yet those in the exhibit who wished to prevent whites from being seen in too intimate a setting with blacks only supported racism. Small wonder that this nation has taken such an image-beating internationally.

Jean and I formulated a plan. After the exhibit closed, we would jump ship from the flight back to the States and go to Paris and be married. We confided our plans to several of our fellow performers and word eventually got back to those in charge.

Leonard Hankin, an official of the exhibit and an executive at Bergdorf Goodman in New York, approached Jean and me backstage. He explained that there is a long waiting period for aliens wishing to be married in France, and his alternate suggestion was that we marry in Moscow. He was a personal friend of Llewellyn Thompson, the United States ambassador to the Soviet Union, and could quickly work out a nice wedding for us.

We approved of the suggestion, although it would be a disappointment for our families in the States, who eagerly awaited our return. Jean and I were married in a civil-court ceremony in Moscow. Our names were added to an official ledger, according to Soviet law, and some unintelligible Russian words, read by a clerk, were pronounced over us.

The wedding was attended by the members of the fashion-

136

pavilion group, plus a corps of United States reporters assigned to cover the show. A story about the event, and an accompanying photograph, appeared the following day in the *New York Times*. After the ceremony, we were invited to the American embassy, where a minister read our vows in English. That evening there was a gala reception at the sumptuous residence of Ambassador Thompson. Jean wore the fabulous gown from the exhibit, and I was decked out in a tuxedo made for me to wear in the show—a service to poetic justice.

The party was marvelous, complete with a receiving line, candlelight, great food, dignitaries, the press, and Soviet officials. Jean was presented with a baby doll by a Russian official, "to hold you over until the real thing comes along." There were a string quartet of musicians and mountains of caviar—the works!

It seemed that every thirty seconds, a Russian would stand and toast, *"Gorka!"* Everyone would rise and applaud, while Jean and I drank a shot of pure Russian vodka through linked arms.

We moved out of the Leningradskaya Hotel to honeymoon in the Hotel Nacional, in Red Square. The next day we telephoned the United States and broke the glad tidings to our families. They were elated and disappointed.

As a wedding present, we were granted a few days' vacation from the fashion exhibit, freeing us to wander around Moscow. We saw the famous mausoleum where the perfectly preserved bodies of Stalin and Lenin are on view. We visited Saint Basil's Cathedral and stopped in the Soviet answer to R. H. Macy's—the GUM department store. We toured the Kremlin with the famed American photographer David Douglas Duncan as our guide. (Duncan was visiting Moscow to film the fabulous Kremlin jewels.)

I was startled to see the excess of the czar's wealth on display. There was a beautiful enclosed sleigh, inside which was a handsomely jeweled pot-bellied stove. The seats were covered in

137

ermine, and other furs adorned the floor. The horses that drew this royal sleigh wore jewel-encrusted bridles and harnesses. Small wonder that the monarchy was overthrown by a peasant majority who were living from hand to mouth. The exhibit is a testament to gluttony and enforced privilege.

During our stay in Moscow, there was another newsmaking event. Vice-President Richard Nixon arrived to tour the United States exhibit. Secret Service men were stationed everywhere. Tension heightened when Nixon toured Moscow with Soviet Premier Nikita Khrushchev, who was accompanied by an even larger contingent of the KGB.

Khrushchev had made an impression at the United Nations in New York when he removed his shoe and pounded on the table during a session of the General Assembly. Now, on his own turf, the Soviet leader strode along with the taller Nixon, dressed in his familiar dark blue suit. Nixon's step was tentative and his smile frozen. Nixon never radiated warmth and love.

The pair moved through the exhibit until they arrived at the domestic-living pavilion, where, amid a swarm of police, press, and Soviet citizens, they engaged in the historic debate through interpreters. The essence of the argument concerned Nixon's attempt to make Khrushchev see that American technology was more advanced than that of the U.S.S.R. Khrushchev insisted that it wouldn't remain that way for long; he declared that the Soviet Union was younger than the United States and capable of catching up, if it was in fact behind.

Nixon pointed to a modern stove in a simulated kitchen area, which Nikita dismissed with a wave of the hand and went on to describe the superiority of Soviet tractors. It seemed to me to be less of a debate than a media event in which both contestants jockeyed for the winner's circle in the press coverage.

I busily rolled my 8-millimeter motion-picture camera when the entourage passed, nearly running us over. My film shows only bedlam, with just the tops of the two statesmen's heads visible above the crowd.

Jean and I met several news correspondents from the major networks in the United States. I had no idea then that they would eventually become my colleagues. We were interviewed by Bob Considine, the Hearst syndicated columnist who was in the Soviet Union doing a string of reports for his radio series, *Tempo*. He asked about Jean and me and how we had become part of the exhibit. He was interested in our impressions of the U.S.S.R. as compared with the United States. The tape ended with praise for the United States as a democracy where two anonymous black Americans could be thrust into the world spotlight. I recall feeling that we had been trumped.

I met several black expatriate Americans, including the brother of Paul Robeson's wife, Eslanda. He seemed quite happy in the Soviet Union, where he remained for the rest of his life.

We also met several Africans. One I will not forget was named Osman, from the Sudan. He ran up to me, talking excitedly in his language and smiling broadly. I didn't understand a word he said. I later discovered that he had mistaken me for one of his countrymen. I thought then, as I do now, that my ancestral line might trace back to Osman's country. We became fast friends and talked for many hours about race problems in the United States. He was concerned, sympathetic, and angry.

We visited the African students' club at the University of Leningrad and met many other beautiful African brothers and sisters. One African had jet-black skin; yet his eyes were sky-blue. They all were keenly aware of the civil rights movement in the United States.

Malcolm X later pointed out that if the struggle had been called the *human*-rights movement, it would have received massive support on an international basis. This may be why the American media played up the movement as being a civil rights struggle.

Calling the issue one of civil rights implied that it was localized, confined to the boundaries of the nation involved, limiting outside intervention, including that of the United Nations.

The blacks in Moscow were on fire about African independence. There was talk of revolution, and some of it was beyond my unsophisticated ken. I came to realize how backward most of my generation was regarding world events. Much of the blame can possibly be placed within the black race. However, blame must justifiably be laid on the deficient educational system of this country.

CHAPTER 15

The key to being an effective media person is involvement in the community. The pressures and seductions of TV can lure one away from the black and poor communities, when there is a real need to remain actively in touch with events there. Success can draw one away from the roots of one's race.

Success can leave little time for visits to Harlem or Bedford-Stuyvesant. You find you've been telling your secretary to screen callers from the old neighborhood. "Tell them anything—just so I don't have to talk to them."

You catch yourself having breakfast, lunch, and dinner with people who are not necessarily interested in what you should be about. They are "nice people." They like you, admire you, advise you. You are invited to their parties and meet plenty of "interesting" people who also find you "interesting."

Advances are made; business offers are extended. You make rationalizations to justify the drift away from the foundations of being black in America today. "After all," you say, "I can't limit myself to the race issue forever. There are other stories to cover in the news. I want to rise above the issue of blackness."

You sit, black as night, rationalizing that you wish to "rise above" your race. You talk "humanism," but the nagging

141

thought, deep in the recesses of your conscience, says that you are really looking for an escape. No matter how you may preen and prance about being black, you find yourself increasingly comfortable with whites and, in direct proportion, less comfortable with blacks. You find yourself saying that you don't want to go to Harlem to cover a disturbance. In conversation with whites, you say, "I don't know what those people want."

It is easy to slip away. Moreover, those around you in TV-land become uneasy if you continually mention the issue of race. For their comfort, and yours, you begin to relate to only those issues that concern whites, engaging in endless dialogue over intracorporate maneuvers, restaurants, resorts, talent, tax shelters, ratings, and the stock market. You gravitate to the in spots around town—discos, expensive restaurants, bars, and posh apartments.

Where you once were uptight about drugs, you now smile tolerantly as cocaine is passed around at jet-set parties. Your taste in music changes—you catch yourself digging the latest rock sounds and listening less to serious black music.

The transformation is almost complete. Your blackness is eroding. Your militancy is gone. You are no longer angry. You don't want to fight. You are reluctant to be an "irritant."

Malcolm X spoke of this process, using coffee as an analogy. "Black coffee is strong," he would say, "so in order to cool it out, you integrate it with cream. Where it once was hot, it has become cool. Once it was strong, and now it is weak. It used to wake you up; now it will put you to sleep."

Working for the so-called big time can draw you away from the cradle of your being—the black community. Community activism is tiring and endless. It goes on all day, and the pace picks up when the sun goes down. Contact comes through the telephone. I am glad we get so many calls, but sometimes it is difficult to find time to turn out the weekly program.

In the evening, there might be a meeting with black leaders who

142

want to inform me of their actions on an unofficial basis. These meetings are valuable because we are also able to critique each other. I hear about the quality of my work at these sessions—the good and the bad. What I leave out is mentioned, and I am praised for what I include. I am thus able to pinpoint for black community leaders what I think they can do to enhance their images and move closer to their goals. I can explain why some incident or event didn't get good news coverage and how that can be corrected. We discuss the best times to hold a press conference and how to satisfy the different needs of print reporters, radio reporters, and TV reporters.

In my view, there is nothing subversive or wrong about what goes on during these sessions, especially knowing that my white colleagues powwow on a regular basis with powerful white elected officials and private individuals.

Even more valuable than the meetings with community leaders are the chats I have on the street with plain folk. I often find more wisdom and insight in what these anonymous people have to say than in what I hear from the leadership. They aren't trying to impress anyone; they only want to share what's on their minds.

There is a high level of sophistication in the remarks of the people I speak with on the street. They discuss a wide variety of subjects. Their analysis of Africa, of the American system, and of drug traffic is valuable. I always come away from such impromptu conversations better informed, even when I talk with winos, junkies, and prostitutes. Maybe even more so, in their cases, because they are *out there* and have a unique insight into America. In moving narcotics, pushers brush shoulders with the "cream" of society, and in prostitution, they see whites in a far different light than "respectable."

I recall an interview I had with a stunning young sister who had worked for a year in a plush brothel on Manhattan's upper East Side. She revealed still another aspect of our society. Some of the

143

most bigoted whites have a passionate appetite for sexual contact with black men and women. While practicing racism and racial bias in the executive suites, they indulge in bizarre sexual exercises with blacks who sell their bodies. She told me that there were ten gorgeous women working in the brothel, but that she was the only black. What was strange about her story was that she claimed never to have had sexual intercourse with any of her clients, although she was the star attraction of the penthouse.

Her clientele included some of the wealthiest and most influential men and women in New York City, and they were exclusively white. Some of the men visited her for subjugation, not fornication. They wanted to be humiliated, degraded, and defiled.

Some customers brought men's clothes for her to wear while they donned women's clothes. She was asked to scream crude obscenities at them, and for this treatment, her customers gladly paid the highest prices. After an hour or two of this sickness, the clients left in their waiting limousines, to be driven back to their executive suites downtown, from which they conducted business and politics that affect the entire nation.

This beautiful young woman had a long look at the underbelly of society. Hearing of her experiences helped me to see more realistically the politicians and executives who appeared at news conferences, often pompously discussing moral issues.

Young people teach me a great deal. They are always quick to tell you about yourself. They'll tell you off in a minute and have an uncanny knack of spotting a phony.

I have spent much time in the South Bronx, an area widely publicized as being the spawning ground for dozens of vicious youth gangs. I have met with several gang leaders, not with cameras and bright lights, but just to talk. Their insights about what they are involved in, and why, are revelatory.

Their opinions of the police, politicians, the government, and

144

the media are fascinating. I cannot excuse or condone some of the crimes they commit, but they force one to indict those in this country who are motivated by greed and have forced these youths into destructive behavior through deprivation.

Finally, there are the older folk. I enjoyed many glorious hours with Louis Michaux, proprietor of the famous Harlem book store known as The House of Common Sense and Proper Propaganda, before his death. Every publisher who released a book about blacks automatically sent him a reading copy. Michaux had been heavily involved in the Garvey movement and the black-nationalist movement that emerged from it. He was a source of rare information, and leaders, scholars, and students visited his store and shared and received knowledge.

Michaux would frequently take me downstairs into the basement where he kept his treasures—books and photographs nearly impossible to find elsewhere. He steered me to the very books I needed when I was arming myself for battles in the field of journalism.

From Michaux's generous wit and wisdom, and from the talks I had with other older blacks, I learned the lessons of humor and humility. They taught me not to take myself too seriously but to be serious about my enemies and my work. They also taught me that no matter how original or brilliant a thought seemed, someone had already come up with it.

I learned that during the twenties, the members of a group of intellectuals in Harlem pooled their money and sent their own black delegate-reporter to cover the League of Nations conference in Geneva. There existed, even then, a sophisticated political awareness of the inadequacies of mass journalism. They saw the importance of having their own news information about important events.

I also learned about John Russwurm and Samuel Cornish, two black men who, with their own meager funds, founded the first black newspaper in the United States, called *Freedom's Journal*, in 1827.

I once had a long and close relationship with the late Doctor Arthur Logan, who had been a family physician when I was small. In later years, he was a friend to the black struggle. Through him, I learned what it is to be truly unselfish. He treated patients in his office knowing that they would not be able to pay his fee. On the day of his death, he had made a house call.

Doctor Logan was a friend of the civil rights movement and lent his home as a meeting place in which the leaders of the movement could formulate strategy and relax. He fed them, counseled them, and donated his medical skill when needed. He also contributed - large amounts of money to the cause. He could have been a high-society doctor, with wealthy clients, but he stuck to treating the needy.

Doctor Logan's great example of charity, gentleness, and lack of ego were vital elements in my instruction as a human being. He trusted me and stood by me through many personal tribulations. I hope I have justified his faith in me, and his trust. There is an African tradition of reverence for elders that stirs in my bones.

I feel sad when I witness youngsters who not only fail to respect the elderly, but who assault them. These confused and desperate teenagers are, in a sense, committing suicide. To brutalize the elders of your tribe is to violate your history. Without our elders, we are nothing. What is past is prologue. The elderly have seen it all and have done and tried everything we think about and try to do. It would be worthwhile to listen to what they have to say. Why can't young people see that their elders can save them a lot of steps in life?

Many aspects of the black community have sustained me. By being active in the life of the community, I have kept my balance. My most powerful story ideas have sprung from my contacts there. There are fights and differences of opinion, and charlatans exist among blacks and must be dealt with. But there are also wellsprings of knowledge, talent, spirit, and fresh ideas that have kept me afloat and urged me onward.

CHAPTER 16

What can the future bring? I see many things. Television will have an even greater dominance in the lives of the people of the world. Tomorrow's generation will spend more time watching TV. The quality of television will remain essentially the same. TV fare will continue to serve the interests of business people rather than those of viewers.

There will be a more intensive use of commercials and in more innovative ways, although today's commercials are lethal enough. They not only whet buying appetites, but also manufacture cruel associations in the minds of those watching.

Gerrie Wilson, an expert in early-childhood research, told me of black children who have taken to tying up their heads in yellow bandanas in an effort to be Farrah Fawcett look-alikes. I have also heard of black male children who fantasize about marrying the Bionic Woman when they grow up.

A child psychologist told me of treating disturbed children and hearing a distraught child express the wish that he and his family could spend more time at MacDonald's. When asked why, the child said it was because the commercials always showed the father hugging the mother and both parents hugging the children. To the child in therapy, everyone on the restaurant commercial seemed to be happy and loving, unlike his real-life family.

Far too many subliminal messages are woven into commercials. Take for an illustration the theme of selfishness. Several commercials encourage viewers to focus attention on self rather than to cultivate a concern for others, which is the key to a healthy society. "Be good to yourself . . ." "You've come a long way, baby . . ." "You deserve a break today. . . ." Department stores and shopping malls are crammed with people whose eyes glitter as they rush from counter to counter, obeying the directives of TV commercials to buy, buy, buy.

Fat people try to look thin; dark people try to look light; light people try to look darker; poor people try to buy enough objects to appear wealthy. Most of us are in dire financial straits. We carry on, only a step ahead of our creditors. How often have you caught yourself saying that you need something you don't really need, but merely *want?*

We are sold the cruel implications that the acquisition of material things will enhance our manhood, our womanhood, and our sexuality and also solve most of our problems. The family skits showing how problems are solved through the acquisition of a new car, for instance, or a more expensive brand of coffee, or life insurance, all end with the image of a happy couple, safe and loving, snuggling together in satisfaction. Happiness is achieved at last—with the product wedged between the lucky owners.

If you think you have escaped the influence of this media conditioning, consider how many hours of television you watch daily. Three hours per day is conservative. That is twenty-one hours per week; ninety hours per month; one thousand and ninety-five hours per year. At least ten percent of that viewing time is spent on commercials—also a conservative estimate. You spend at least one hundred hours per year watching television commercials, which is probably more time than the average person gets as vacation time from a job!

The barrage of commercials falsely conditions the public into thinking that acquisition of material goods will answer the problems that plague us. It teaches us that certain textures and colors of hair are ideal and that husband-wife relations can be enhanced by eliminating ring around the collar.

For the poorest among us, the slum dweller, this conditioning is psychological sadism. It dangles a sirloin steak before millions of people who cannot afford hamburger. The people who have spent their days creating the commercials bemoan the fact that there are so many muggings, robberies, and killings on the streets; yet they refuse to consider their own form of psychological mugging.

If current commercials are often evil in their effect, tomorrow's will be even more so. Manufacturers rely less on quality to sell their goods and more on the huckstering of TV promotion. The quality-control budget is slashed to increase the advertising budget. The results are evident, as in the auto-tire manufacturer who spent a fortune advertising tires that "gr-r-r-ipped the road" but were found to have lowered the safety standards of the tire in the process. A heavily advertised compact car was little more than a bomb on wheels because of its faulty gasoline tank.

Haven't we had enough of blondes lying seductively on automobiles, running through open fields, riding bareback in the throes of ecstasy over a new brand of deodorant? What does a blonde in a slinky dress have to do with a Sanyo stereo set?*

The injury to blacks is twofold. The pitch is rooted along sexist lines that degrade women and presume that men can value merchandise only in sexual terms. The sexual pitch is racist, in consistently glorifying white blondness. Some blacks have once

*"Portrayal of Women and Minorities in Television Programming
1. The Federal Communications Commission should conduct an inquiry and proposed rulemaking in which it would investigate the relationship between the network programming decisionmaking process, the resulting portrayal of minorities and women, and the impact of these portrayals on viewers."
(Window Dressing on the Set—An Update, from a report of the United States Commission on Civil Rights.)

again taken to straightening their naturally kinky hair. These days they refer to the process as "relaxing," and the texture that is sought is "lustra-silk." Our women are using skin bleaches, but now the ideal is termed "skin blush."

If commercials continue to increase the appeal of luxury items in a nation where the most fundamental needs are lacking for one-third of the citizens, then, as the old Astaire-Rogers song goes: "There will be trouble ahead. . . ."

Each Christmas is a season of frustration and humiliation to millions of disadvantaged Americans, a large part of whom are black. They cannot give what their TV sets command them to give to their loved ones. They can't show they really love them, in the way commercials dictate it is necessary to do.

Divorce and family courts across the nation report that most disputes in the home revolve around money and consumerism. Men feel themselves less manly because TV commercials have tied masculinity to buying power. Men have been taught to believe that the only way to show love is to buy something.

The big future impact of TV is in international telecasting. American TV networks are selling more old programs to emerging Third World nations. American businesses—and the nationless multinationals—are operating in such countries, and buying up air time. The world as a whole is increasingly joining in the chorus of *I Love Lucy* and *Father Knows Best*, "brought to them by the makers of . . ."

The good old American way of life has planted roots abroad. It is now possible to travel overseas without ever really leaving this country. You fly aboard an American airline, which serves American food and shows American-made movies. You can arrive in Cairo and be driven in an American limousine to the sumptuous Cairo Hilton. In your room overlooking the city, your dinner is brought, featuring standard American food. Or you can journey downstairs to the dining room and eat the same

152

fare, while a group of Egyptian musicians play the latest disco sounds from the United States.

In the hotel lobby are a boutique, a beauty salon, and a pharmacy, all chock full of the familiar American products and magazines. Back in the room, the radio offers several local stations that play "your kind" of (American) music, or you can flip on the television set (American brand) and view the friendly canned episodes of *Gunsmoke* and, if you're lucky, *The Jeffersons*.

If you do find the heart to venture forth into the foreign streets, you will find a surprisingly large number of kids wearing American jeans and carrying portable radios that blast the Top Ten from American rock-music charts. During a bus tour, you can listen to a disco group playing at the base of the Pyramids. After fourteen days abroad you exclaim, as you land at JFK Airport, "Boy, it sure is good to be back home!"

Foreigners are now having the American way of life brought to them. They are just as unaware as American citizens that the things advertised as "the best in life" are out of reach and unavailable to the average person.

Satellites facilitate the global transmission of American television programming. Much of the world's oldest culture is in shreds thanks to Americanization. Cities of the world are jammed with people who pour in from the countryside in search of blue- or white-collar jobs and the "better way of life."

In several foreign lands, governments complain that the basic vocations of farming and carpentry are out of favor with the upcoming generations. These countries have begun to import agricultural products from the United States. We are the OPEC of the world's food supply and the world's largest exporter of food products. In countries like Vietnam, rice was once the basic food. Now the Vietnamese import this staple from the United States. Sam Yette writes brilliantly about this in his valuable book *The Choice*.

In Jamaica, the land of my most immediate roots, the same problem exists. The values of the young people have been turned away from the vocations that Jamaica needs most. Jamaican youths are choking the cities of Kingston and Montego Bay, looking for office jobs and their attendent prestige. Unfortunately, these jobs do not exist in adequate numbers to satisfy the demand.

Jamaica needs for its young people to remain in the country to tend the rich farmland, but their values are elsewhere, and in frustration, they turn to crime and drugs.

Third World youths can no longer be controlled by their parents, churches, or schools. They are, in fact, out of control. The problems of juvenile misbehavior familiar to Americans have spread, as the impact of television has spread.

An example of my concern surfaced in a film shown on *Like It Is*, called *Bottle Babies*. This film tells how the Nestlé Company embarked on an intensive media campaign in Third World countries, especially Africa, to market bottled formula. Posters cover these countries extolling the prestige and glamour of this "modern" method of feeding infants. Radio commercials preach not only that the formula is good for the babies, but that there is something old-fashioned and uncivilized about breast-feeding. This advertising campaign reached even the most remote villages.

On *Like It Is*, we showed how the people came to heed that message and hurried to buy the bottled formula. Unfortunately, the new customers could not read the directions, in English, on the label detailing the correct method of preparation. The mothers didn't know that exact mixtures were critical in order for the baby to be properly nourished. The mothers merely added enough formula to water to give a milklike consistency and fed that to their infants. The directions emphasized that the formula was to be mixed with carefully sterilized water. Not understanding this, the women filled their bottles from the rivers.

It was heart-rending to see African women, whose breasts were full of rich, nourishing milk, feeding the diluted and inadequate formula to their children. The rate of infant mortality has risen drastically in the areas where bottle feeding has been successfully touted. Governments have appropriated funds to mount an advertising counter-campaign, which warns families of the dangers of improper bottle feeding.

When *Like It Is* decided to air this powerfully affecting film expose, I contacted the formula company and offered them rebuttal time. A spokesman limousined to our studio from Westchester County and delivered a carefully written statement for *me* to read on the air! I asked him if he didn't want to deliver the statement himself, but he smiled nervously and refused.

A boycott has been launched against such destructive marketing practices, and I hope that the company will heed the criticisms.

But what of other companies that exploit consumers in Third World countries, such as the tobacco companies which sell cancer- and heart-attack-inducing cigarettes with the Surgeon General's health warning removed from the package? What about the ads, so effective in poorer communities, that create a demand for junk foods that contain little nutritional value and are full of dangerous chemicals and risky levels of starch and sugar?

I don't look forward to a world where everything is standardized. Only equality and humanism should be culturally universal. It is not my desire for the cultures of the world to become Americanized, either. Americans have much to learn from other countries about values. Television can aid in building world human values or contribute to their destruction, depending on controls put into effect now.

African nations can seldom file stories from their point of view for the United Press-International, Reuters, or the Associated Press, although reports from these agencies feed the world's news channels. News from these nations is gathered by reporters and editors who are neither African nor Third World. There is a built-

155

in bias in the material, regardless of how well intentioned the reporters are.

This sort of bias shows itself in reporting in a variety of ways. For instance, South Africa is seldom referred to as "racist South Africa." Acts of rebellion against white oppression in that country are always termed "terrorist activities."

The regime of Ian Smith was hardly ever referred to as illegitimate, which it was in fact. Little emphasis is placed on the enormous amount of economic support the United States gave the racist regimes in Zimbabwe and Azania (Rhodesia and South Africa).

There is another dimension to my concern over world communication and the proper dissemination of information to all the peoples of the world. What about news traveling among Third World countries? When an event occurs in Zimbabwe, the reports that are broadcast to Jamaica, for example, are made by reporters of European descent. The possible serious misunderstandings that might arise could cause a breech between nations. A statement by Julius Nyerere, the president of Tanzania, could be misreported and therefore considered insulting or threatening to another African nation.

Such things have actually happened, encouraging dangerous breeches in political relationships between two countries that had not formerly been hostile. For example, when Tanzanian president Julius Nyerere ordered his troops into action against Idi Amin Dada's forces in Uganda, several nations reacted negatively toward Tanzania because early news reports had not mentioned that Uganda had actually attacked Tanzania first.

There is little direct news communication among neighboring African countries. A news report of an event taking place in Ghana is not directly transmitted to the Ivory Coast. Instead, it is filed by a reporter of European descent, wired to Paris or Rome, and then transmitted to the Ivory Coast. During this process, the report passes through several hands, none of them black. By the time the report reaches the Ivory Coast, it could be far from factual.

All communication among nations of color is monitored. Telephone calls from one African nation to another are not direct but go to a European city and are then routed back to the African country being called. A short air hop from Nigeria to the Cameroon is all but impossible. The airline carries passengers to Paris and then back to the African continent.

Third World nations have begun to respond to the problem; they increasingly confer with each other on these crucial matters. There should be an independent network operating among Third World nations, owned and controlled by people of color. An independent news service would also be valuable in strengthening the universal position of Third World countries.

It would be refreshing to hear a progressive African commentary on pertinent African issues. This input would offer perspectives that might alter world political policies. If the American people had a wider view on world issues, they might compel their leaders to change our suicidal direction.

It is sad that official United States policy has almost always favored the wrong side. This country refused to recognize the Ho Chi Minh government in Vietnam in 1955, even though their Declaration of Independence was modeled after ours. Instead, we created and supported a series of corrupt puppet regimes that brutalized and exploited the Vietnamese people.*

* "I think the major problem with foreign correspondents in Third World countries—I've seen this in Africa, I've seen this in Vietnam, I've seen this in South America—the major problem is that they do what one calls 'American Embassy reporting.' They get off the plane, they go to the American Embassy, and they sit for two hours being briefed by these officials . . . . then file their stories. Frequently, they never talk to a local person. Frequently, they will be scared to death to talk to a local person. They'll go and stay, as most of us do, in the best hotels in these places . . . and who stays in these best hotels, but the colonials who are still there, still running the plantations up in the bush, who have all kinds of colonial attitudes about the local people. Now these are the people you'll meet in the bar and around the swimming pool, and all too often, these are the people

The Central Intelligence Agency spent millions of our dollars to overthrow a legally elected government in Chile and install a military regime comprised of one of the worst bands of torturers and murderers in the bloody history of Latin America. The wife of folk guitarist Victor Jara, who was detained in the Chilean national stadium with five-thousand other prisoners, testified that her husband's fingers were broken, after which he was forced to play the guitar for the amusement of his captors. This atrocity was performed before, in their boredom, they put fifty-seven bullets into his body.

American public opinion is easily manipulated. There was relatively little protest when the president of Chile, Gossens Allende, was assassinated and his government was overthrown at our direction. The torture and murder that followed could have had the seal: APPROVED BY THE U.S.A. on it. Perhaps an enlightened American public would not have allowed this to happen.

If the United States could boycott Cuba, they could certainly do the same to South Africa. The United States tried to cut off all world credit to Chile under the Allende government and could have done the same thing to the illegal Ian Smith regime in so- called Rhodesia.

Ian Smith was invited to visit the United States by a cartel of private businessmen and members of Congress. President Carter approved of the State Department clearing of Smith's visa. Not a discouraging word was heard from any member of Congress. Smith came to this country and was wined and dined in Washington and New York. If the media could expose the policies and

who contribute to the story that this foreign correspondent writes. Now it doesn't stop there, because once it's written or once it is telecast and Washington sees it, that does indeed influence the State Department in Washington and they in turn influence their people back on the grounds. So you've got a rather incestuous round robin of highly suspect kinds of information.

"I think one thing one has to note about the American press is that the mass media [do] follow the lead of the State Department, and wherever the State Department puts a priority, the American media will generally follow."

(Tom Johnson, *New York Times* correspondent, October 23, 1977, on WABC-TV's *Like It Is.*)

practices of an Idi Amin Dada of Uganda, how could they remain mute regarding Ian Smith?

What would mass American public reaction be to the realization that the same United States banks that are choking the American public and several American cities, including New York, are also extending credit and cash to the racist regimes (not governments) in Zimbabwe and Azania?

The news carriers have the power and ability to make friends look like enemies and enemies look like friends.

Malcolm X once brilliantly pointed out how, during World War II, the press correctly identified the Germans and the Japanese as our enemies and the Russians and the Chinese as our friends. Then, after the war, they reversed this pronouncement, making the Germans and the Japanese our allies and the Russians and the Chinese our enemies.

We might closely examine the corrupt relationship between the news media in America and the various secret agencies of government—the CIA and the FBI roles in manipulating mass media. It might be healthy for the public to see how the news media and outside forces have created and controlled news stories that are often outright lies.

I conducted an in-depth interview with a former Central Intelligence Agency official, John Stockwell, who gave explicit information on how the CIA molds public opinion in the United States concerning events taking place elsewhere in the world. Stockwell spoke about his type of outside government influence on the press as "commonplace."

Martin Luther King, Jr., used the quote: "No lie can live forever," and this bit of wisdom is true. There are countless lies fed to the American public that will eventually be exposed. There will be more Watergates and Koreagates. Knowing the truth can only strengthen us. Access to news means that we all get a fair variety of information on what's happening in this world.

In a recent example of misreporting, riots were claimed to have taken place in Jamaica in early 1979. An article in *Newsweek* was headlined, "Showdown in the Sun," accompanied by a photograph of an armored tank in a Jamaican street. The implication was that a reign of terror was underway.

I went to Jamaica to see for myself and found that the "riots" had been blown far out of proportion. The spate of reports came from a single correspondent, and there was no "showdown in the sun," as the headline shouted. Instead, a series of island-wide demonstrations against a proposed gasoline-price increase took the form of roadblocks, which caused some inconvenience to everyone in Kingston and Montego Bay. The tank in the photograph wasn't rumbling through the streets but was being used by the government to haul away the blockades.

While in Jamaica on that trip, I found a good deal of concern among native citizens over the economy of their country. They continue to have a rough time. The riot stories were obviously designed to cripple Jamaica's revived tourism by frightening off potential visitors. There might not have been such a scare if the news reports had been presented from another perspective.

CHAPTER 17

At the risk of compromising my objectivity as a reporter, I have an obligation to express my thoughts about Jamaica, which is, after all, the birthplace of several of my family generations. I have a deep attachment to this island because of the roots that link me to my enduring African lineage.

I often try to imagine my father, with his physical and moral strength, as the African ancestor who was kidnapped and brought to Jamaica. If that historical ancestor was anything like my father, it would have required the most strenuous means to take him captive. Only the most extreme methods, over a protracted period of time, could have made him a captive, and then in body only. In fact, I have discovered that my African ancestor was a rebellious "Maroon" in Jamaica.

The more years I add to my life, the stronger my thoughts grow toward that African ancestor, whose face I will never know and whose name is lost in time. Since I do know that Jamaica is the first soil reached by my family after leaving Africa, I am very deeply involved with the island's history and in what is happening there today.

Jamaica's problems are numerous and have many aspects. I believe that they all stem from a common denominator—colonialism. Jamaica has always struggled against colonial domination, and the struggle continues today, even though the island is no longer a formal colony. Jamaica became an "independent" nation in 1962 but has yet to become fully divested of the ravages of its cruel colonial past. Though the physical presence of Britain is no longer there, British economic domination is still a powerful reality. England not only continues to exert great influence over Jamaica, but does so in concert with the United States. The island has long tried to tear away from foreign domination, correctly defined as neocolonialism.

The banking system in Jamaica is controlled from the outside by Western nations. No nation can exist on modern terms without an independent banking system that permits the establishment of trade and raises credit. Even the simplest international trade purchase between two nations cannot take place smoothly without the existence of a banking system.

When a tanker arrives in a Jamaican harbor carrying oil from an American refining company, payment is made through a sophisticated international banking system, which involves letters of credit and other complex financial maneuvers. The Jamaican government might issue a payment draft that draws funds from its own cash reserves. This payment draft then goes to a bank—usually American or British—which in turn issues another payment draft to the oil-refining company.

That, in principle, is how international purchases are paid for, although the procedure can be infinitely more complicated. But the role of the bank is critical. If the government of Jamaica is low on cash reserves, it can apply to the international bank for a credit advance in order to receive the goods. The bank then has the option of granting or refusing the line of credit. If the decision is positive, the bank then pays the oil company and extends to Jamaica a given period of time in which to repay the credit advance.

Banks in Jamaica have long been unwilling to extend much credit to the Jamaican government. This is because Jamaica has suffered internal economic problems that have caused it to have a bad credit rating with international banks.

Jamaica has sought to reverse the old national standard of economic and political values to give poor people top priority. This change has caused vast expenditures on social programs, such as schools, hospitals, housing, and other improvements in the living standards of the native Jamaicans. Heavy outlays in these areas are not capital earning, at least not in a short-term investment-return sense. Jamaica, therefore, has been accumulating a large debt in trying to realize the success of these social programs. The banks have grown increasingly unhappy, preferring that Jamaica spend huge sums of money on hotels, beach improvements, and other tourist-related projects. Investments in these areas would realize a faster return on revenues, and the many American hotels that operate in Jamaica and have close investment ties with the banks would reap handsome profits.

The ongoing struggle of these international banks to get Jamaica to reverse its spending priorities has been resisted by Prime Minister Michael Manley. These banking interests argue that if Manley would set aside his policies for a time and support the development of foreign investments, he could help his people at some later date. Manley argues that this has been the philosophy of the past. The attitude of giving foreign interests priority over the needs of the poor have consigned most Jamaicans to unremitting poverty for decades.

Faced with this resistance, bankers have begun to tighten the screws, and credit is hard to get. Jamaica has been forced to seek assistance from the World Bank and the International Monetary Fund, among other financial outlets. These agencies are controlled by the same banking institutions that have been tightening the screws. Many essential materials are now difficult to import.

163

Several banking institutions have shut down their offices on the island.

An important sector of middle-class Jamaicans have lost jobs, have become frightened, and are pulling up stakes and migrating to the United States and Canada. A cry has gone up in some quarters of Jamaica that Manley is a communist, which is untrue. The prime minister is caught between very powerful economic pincers, while crusading to relieve the centuries of poverty in his land.

With the loss of the Jamaican middle class, little support is forthcoming for Manley's reforms. The middle class plays a crucial role in Jamaican society, being composed of the skilled and educated citizens who possess the best potential for assisting in uplifting the poor.

The international media have also been giving Jamaica a very bad press. The "communist" label is sticking, and tourism has dropped sharply. Many Jamaican citizens who left as a result of the "communist" scare have exacerbated Jamaica's problems by taking their money out of the country.

Manley has worked hard to earn the love and support of the poor in his country, despite opposition and lack of assistance. Remote mountain areas of the country now have schools, electricity, health services, and other utilities where none previously existed. Thousands of Jamaican youths are now the first in their families to receive higher education, and literacy levels have risen. Workers have acquired a new and inspiring dignity. Better housing is available to the poor. In only seven years, Jamaican living standards have dramatically changed. Nevertheless, grave problems remain.

I criticize the manner in which American-influenced international bankers have strangled the Jamaican economy while extending unlimited credit to the most illicit regimes on earth. In spite of this nation's expressed hatred for the Soviet Union,

164

America's prime banking institution, the Chase Manhattan Bank, operates a branch in Moscow's Red Square. Bankers continue to extend credit to the Republic of South Africa, and the devotion and support of David Rockefeller for the former shah of Iran, a brutal and despotic ruler, has caused world concern. American bankers have had the same ugly track record in Nicaragua, the Philippines, South Korea, and South Vietnam, all under the auspices of being committed to justice and human rights.

The international banking community, while under the leadership of my former employer, Chase Manhattan Bank, should be viewed as demonic despots with little integrity or legitimacy. These banks hold several major American cities in the grip of a high-interest debt that will be as difficult to eliminate as it is to pay off a loan shark.

I salute Michael Manley for his uncompromising fight for the human rights of all Jamaican citizens. The strangulation of Jamaica by banking combines must be exposed to the world, and the institutions themselves must be compelled to change their ugly ways.

On June 22, 1980, a plot to overthrow the Manley government was uncovered, and twenty-three people were arrested. As this book goes to press, predictions are that more trouble lies ahead for Manley.

CHAPTER **18**

People who are in distress or who run afoul of the law often call TV news reporters for sanctuary. I receive many such calls whenever I do a story about urban neglect. I may report on a family in Harlem that lives in an all-but-abandoned apartment building with no heat or hot water. Afterward, I usually receive one hundred or more calls from citizens in similar or worse circumstances.

Even more serious are those individuals who break the law and call on a reporter to assist in bargaining with the police. I was once driving to work when a man attempted to hold up the branch of the Chase Manhattan Bank on 135th Street and Fifth Avenue. Police were alerted instantly and arrived at the scene while the man was still inside the bank. When he realized his predicament, the robber barricaded himself inside the bank office, holding several patrons and employees hostage. Police officers were not eager to storm the bank because of the danger to the hostages. A special New York Police Department negotiating team was brought in to establish communications with the man inside and attempt to talk him out of what he was about.

This happened within a very short time, and none of these events were known to me, since I was still on my way to the newsroom. The police team was finally able to converse with the man through a telephone inside the bank. He said he would consider releasing the hostages if he were allowed to surrender safely.

Although the police reassured him of his safety, he was still not convinced, and he finally said that the only way he would surrender was if Gil Noble of *Eyewitness News* escorted him to safety after the hostages had been released.

An account of what was happening had been broadcast over the police radio in the Eyewitness News room. A news camera crew and reporter had been sent to the scene immediately, but with the latest development, a cry went up, "Where is Gil Noble?" I was, in fact, just arriving for work.

When I walked into the newsroom, my co-workers rushed up to me shouting, at the same time pushing me back through the door. I pieced together the story and arrived fifteen minutes later at the scene of the robbery. By that time, the bandit had agreed to allow WCBS reporter Chris Borgen, who was already there, to accompany him to safety. Borgen is a black, was once a policeman, and is crime-investigation reporter for WCBS. The hostages were released, and Borgen escorted the man outside the bank and delivered him to the waiting police.

The visibility of being a reporter encourages demands from many sources. The bank-robbery incident wasn't the only such occasion in my experience. In January 1980, I visited Jamaica with my wife and one of our daughters for a ten-day vacation. John and Grace Killens also joined us on that trip. John Oliver Killens, a well-known writer, and I have been friends for years.

On the last day of a wonderful vacation, I received an urgent phone call from the New York office of *Eyewitness News*. The assignment editor explained that an airplane that had taken off from Atlanta on its way to Kennedy airport had been skyjacked to Havana. The skyjacker was calling for Gil Noble, and the newsroom wanted me to fly to Havana.

As soon as I hung up, the FBI called from Washington with a request that I go to Havana and board the plane in exchange for the hostages. Then, in accordance with the skyjacker's wishes, I was to accompany him on the plane to Teheran.

I explained to the FBI official that I was talking to him from a beach area on the north coast of Jamaica. The only flights I was aware of from Jamaica to Havana left from Kingston, which was several hours distant. In addition, there were only two flights per week between Jamaica and Cuba, neither which left on that day.

My main concern was that I was being asked to risk my life, and I told the agent that I would have to discuss the request with my family, which I did. The consensus was that I shouldn't go. "Something doesn't smell right," someone said.

"You mean that the FBI wants you to exchange yourself for the hostages?" another person said. "No good."

After discussing it for an hour, I received another call, this one from the Miami FBI office. The agent said that if I agreed to go, the FBI would dispatch a Delta Airlines flight from Miami to pick me up in nearby Montego Bay and fly me to Havana. I was to attempt to talk to the skyjacker from the airport control tower and would not be asked to board the plane. If it became necessary for me to do that, the decision would be made at the scene.

The skyjacker was reported to have a pistol and a grenade, but since I was being asked to talk to him from the safety of the control tower, I felt I should go. The newsroom in New York called for my decision, and I explained that I had agreed to go to Havana. They requested a telephone interview with the sky-jacker.

By the time I arrived at the Montego Bay airport, I began to get a sense of the importance of the story. The phones at the desks of every airline had calls waiting for me from news outfits in New York. My name was being paged all over the airport: "Your attention, please. Will Mr. Gil Noble please come to the desk phone at Air Jamaica. You have an urgent call from New York." As I finished one call, I was paged to go to a different airline counter to take another.

The story was getting major play in New York. Many fellow reporters working for other stations wanted to interview me. I understood the desperation of the news media over a major skyjacking story.

Several interviews focused on my feelings about going to Havana. I was asked if I was afraid. How did I feel about facing the possibility of . . . "Well, er, ah . . . you know. How do you feel about it?" After years of being on the other side of the interview, I had become the interviewee.

The plane that was to take me to Havana arrived, and just as I was about to board, I was told that there was still *another* urgent call for me at the terminal. It was the Miami FBI saying that I didn't need to go. The hostages had been released and the skyjacker was in custody. Mercifully, no one had been hurt.

The skyjacker was a young man who did not seem to fit the traditional stereotype of such an offender. Samuel Alden Ingram, Jr., is twenty-eight years old, and he and his wife and baby are from New York. They were in Atlanta on a family visit. At this writing, Ingram is being held by authorities in Cuba. When the crisis ended, and I had returned to New York, Ingram managed to call me from Havana, and I succeeded in interviewing him over the telephone.

Ingram explained that he is a Muslim but not a member of the Nation of Islam or the World Community of Islam. His Muslim name is Ishmael Siraj. He told me that he decided to commit the hijacking because of the convictions of a group of which he is a member. This group, which operates in several cities, wanted the public in the United States and Iran to know that there was support for the Iranian holding of hostages in demand for the

170

return of the Shah to stand trial for his crimes.

I asked Ingram why he had committed the skyjacking when his wife and child were with him, but he refused to comment. He warned that there would be future actions of this nature. I asked why he had called for me, and he said that he had seen my work on WABC-TV and felt that I could be trusted to bargain in good faith.

The question, therefore, prevails: Should a reporter be exposed to the risk of loss of life as a part of his or her job? In the course of performing this work, jeopardy is almost unavoidable. Each reporter must make a personal decision according to the situation, but I emphasize that police authorities should play a more active role in preventing reporters from being involved in dangerous situations. Reporters are only journalists and have little or no expertise in dealing with criminals. One wrong move could mean the life of the reporter, as well as the hostages, not to mention that of the criminal.

The following is the United Press International dispatch about the January 25, 1980, skyjacking mentioned earlier.

SELF-STYLED MUSLIM FAILS IN CUBA-TO-IRAN HIJACK

MIAMI (UPI)—A gunman traveling with his wife and two daughters hijacked a Delta Airlines jet Friday and forced it to Cuba, where he surrendered after all his hostages sneaked off the plane while he negotiated for a flight to Iran.

"We snuck out the back while he was in the cockpit," said Lynn Martin, 19, of Dallas, one of the 53 passengers aboard Delta Flight 1116.

No one was harmed in the 14 hour ordeal, although Arthur Nerhbass, FBI agent-in-charge in Miami, said "a few are slightly ill. Nothing serious."

The FBI identified the hijacker as Samuel Aldon Ingram, Jr.,

28, of Atlanta. They said he was with his wife and two daughters, aged 3 years and 13 months. All four remained in custody of Cuban authorities.

It was learned that Ingram, who boarded the plane through tight security in Atlanta, took a .25-caliber pistol aboard hidden in his baby's clothes—a ruse recently featured in the "Dick Tracy" comic strip.

While the hijacker was negotiating and his family was sleeping, stewardesses sneaked the passengers off the plane in small groups, using the dumbwaiter that hoists supplies into the cabin. After that, Pilot Donald Vickers said, "the hijacker was convinced to give himself up." There was no struggle, he said, after the man was convinced he had no leverage left.

There were reports Ingram had identified himself as a black Muslim, but Abraham Pasha, Atlanta regional Imam of the World Community of AlIslam in the West, said Ingram was not on the church's register. The group ceased calling itself the Black Muslims years ago and Pasha said "'When he said he was a Black Muslim I knew he wasn't a member of our group."

Atlanta police said they had no record of Ingram.

Flight 1116, which originated in San Francisco and stopped in Dallas, was en route from Atlanta to New York when it was commandeered over Greensboro, N.C., at 1:51 a.m. It reached Jose Marti Airport in Havana at 4:03 a.m. and, after the hijacking was over, flew to Miami. It was to continue on to New York late Friday night.

For nearly 11 hours, the plane sat on the tarmac at Jose Marti in Cuba while the hijacker negotiated for a plane to take him and his family to Tehran. He offered to trade the passengers for Gil Noble, a black reporter for WABC-TV in New York, and an official of the Iranian embassy, who would join them for the flight to the Mideast.

172

CHAPTER 19

Many who read this book may wonder if I hate white people. I must confess that this is a difficult question for me to answer. On one hand, I feel deep resentment for the manner in which the white race in this and other countries has mistreated the people of my race. Yet I cannot say that I hate each and every white person.

I am fundamentally opposed to racism and racist attitudes. How, then, could I in good conscience have a racist attitude? The problem has perhaps best been stated in the past by several great men. Doctor Du Bois said, "The problem of the twentieth century is the problem of the color line." Martin Luther King stated that prejudice and racism infect both the racist and the victim.

As a victim of racism, I have built up a deep layer of scar tissue that often prohibits me from being fully open with whites. On many occasions, I have tried to discard that scar tissue and be open, only to be slapped across the face when I least expected it by a racist action or comment that caused more scar tissue to form.

This situation represents a great loss to me. There are many personal friendships that I fear will never develop—relationships with whites—because of the climate of racism. Many people who

173

are white may be injured by something I do or say, although they may be completely innocent. Sadly, both sides pay the price.

This very passage I write has been drafted several times. The publisher of this book, Lyle Stuart, had a noticeable reaction to the first draft, which read: "I guess most of you who are reading this book think that I don't like white people. I don't." Despite his smile, I could see that he was taken aback when he read my words. We didn't discuss it in any detail, but over the ensuing months of finishing this book, Lyle inevitably joked about my "antiwhite" feelings.

My feelings of resentment against whites are of a collective nature, not individual. I cannot say that I hate all white people, really. I *can* say that I hate racism and all who practice it. I deeply resent a nation that oppresses a group of people based on their color, while at the same time professing to be "the land of the free and the home of the brave."

I have met several whites who have treated me as a human being, which is all any person would ask. I have experienced occasions when a white person went out of the way to be courteous, even though there seemed to be nothing in it for her or him. My feelings are mixed and complex. I cannot lift their burden from my shoulders, because racism is still so much a part of America.

I sometimes sit in my office, sorting through my daily mail, finding much of it praiseworthy, while some is critical. Most of the letters I receive are written in a spirit of goodwill. Then I discover among them the inevitable letter spewing hatred for my race. One letter in particular stated that the wish of the writer was that, before he died, he would have a chance "to kill a nigger." I know that I shouldn't let things like that get to me, but they do. These attacks unleash the deep resentment that has built up in the course of my being bruised and battered as a black in this country.

Something in the attitude of white Americans won't allow

174

them to accept a black organization's expression of its own priorities. This attitude shows up in the manner in which so many whites carry themselves—in their arrogance, their speech, and their eyes. They cannot view a black as an equal.

In a thousand different ways, whites tell black Americans how little they think of us. Contempt isn't always as obvious as with "Bull" Connor or George Lincoln Rockwell or Richard Nixon. It can be as subtle as practiced by Nelson Rockefeller or Jimmy Carter or Ed Koch.

Racism can be as sugar coated as the Supreme Court decision on the Bakke case, which fooled civil rights organizations at first. This hatred can take the form of a taxicab passing a black without stopping, or the slowness in which a certain department in the company you work for responds to a request, in contrast to their response in satisfying a white employee. The cold glaze that comes into some white people's eyes as they meet a black is the typical indication of prejudice.

Some whites might think that blacks don't notice. They think that because blacks laugh with you and joke with you in the corridors, and because you might dine together and even cohabit, blacks are fooled into believing racism doesn't exist. It does.

Some blacks are so hungry for success that they fool even themselves into thinking that the "ice" isn't there. But those who ignore it have made only a superficial adjustment to the situation. Deep, deep inside, they know the real truth—that racist attitudes live on in the collective hearts of white folk.

When one views the madness taking place in the streets of our cities—the evil and senseless acts of violence that are carried out by race against race and within each race—one may understand my prayer for an end to all inhumanity. The best illustration of this is to be found in Tommy's story.

Several years ago, I was in the studio of the black artist Don Miller, who has devoted his artistic life to capturing the black ethic and experience on canvas and in other media. On the walls of his studio hung paintings of such heroes as W. E. B. DuBois, Martin Luther King, Malcolm X, Stokely Carmichael, Fannie Lou Hamer, Mary McLeod Bethune, and others. There were striking paintings of African warriors and children. The entire studio lived and breathed the glory of blackness—except for one picture. In the corner of the studio hung an oil painting of a young white man, which stuck out like a sore thumb. I asked Miller about it, and he smiled and replied, "Oh, that's Tommy."

Miller had come to know Tommy several years earlier. The boy had lived in a rather well-to-do white suburban community. His high school, however, was integrated, and Tommy became friendly with blacks there. He maintained his friendships when he entered college, and every summer he took an apartment in a black community and worked with an "uplift" program. He was so genuine in his concern and manner that he became part of the black community, which looked forward to his return each year.

At the close of one especially productive and successful summer for the program he was associated with, Tommy's fellow worker and close friend became engaged. A stag party was planned, and because Tommy's home was the most spacious, he insisted that the party take place there. It was a relatively mild stag party but a euphoric one, based on the beautiful summer they had all shared.

When the party ended, the guests piled into their cars and set out to get something to eat. Tommy jumped into a convertible, along with three of his black friends. As they headed toward town, Tommy, who was perched on the top of the rear seat, pitched backward as the car hit a bump in the road. He was thrown out of the car and tumbled to the pavement, striking his head as he fell.

The car screeched to a halt and his friends jumped out, ready to go to Tommy's aid. As they tried to revive him, another car approached, driven by a middle-aged white man, whose head was filled with God knows what racial images fostered by our national climate.

As the car neared the accident, Tommy's friends rushed forward to stop the oncoming vehicle from hitting the fallen boy. It was close to one in the morning, and the motorist saw before him three black teenagers waving him down. He panicked and hit the accelerator, swerving around the boys and careering onto the shoulder of the road for several feet, then back onto the road surface, running over Tommy and killing him instantly.

Tommy's funeral was held in the black community where he had worked so hard. The church was packed. Tommy's favorite song, "Respect," by Aretha Franklin, was played, while blacks and whites sat together and wept. After the service, the pallbearers carried Tommy's casket on their shoulders through the black community, while people poured from their homes to join the cortege on its mournful way to the cemetery.

This is an example of how I see prejudice in the United States. It often takes a tragedy to bring the races together in a common purpose. Do I hate whites? It is a question that bears individual answering.

CHAPTER 20

The United States government has spent millions of dollars on studies of black people. Legions of analysts have put us and our communities under microscopes in order to determine why we are the way we are. The *real* problem has never been studied. I propose an in-depth study of *white* folk. I suggest that flotillas of researchers and analysts descend on white American communities to engage in a profound and intensive study of what makes white folk act the way they do. What makes them believe that they are superior to other peoples, despite the evidence of history to the contrary? What makes white folk want to copy things that blacks have devised and created, and then turn around and look down their noses at us?

This study should be conducted by people who are not white. The magnitude of the problem mandates a "Marshall Plan" effort.

Such a study is needed if there is ever to be any peace between the races. Black people have tried every tactic in the ledger to have whites end their racism, and nothing has worked. The integrationist tactics of Martin Luther King and the separationist tactics of the Nation of Islam haven't worked. The bootstrap work ethic of Booker T. Washington and the intellectual-develop-

179

ment program of W.E.B. DuBois have failed just as dismally.

The question of race has dominated my adult conscience. It has affected my maturation process and hampered my emotional development. It blocked my understanding of myself until I was well into adulthood and caused me unending confusion and anger. My heart has often been a furnace of resentment.

Instead of seeking other priorities, I have adopted Garvey's credo: Race first. This has been the only way I have been able to survive in the white-dominated world. To lower the drawbridge would only open myself to serious hurt and injury.

There are times when I forget. Things may go quite well at times in a mostly white work environment. In these periods, I sometimes relax and let down my guard. I unwind; I smile. Then it happens—a sharp punch to my unguarded solar plexus. A white person will do or say something that will set into sharp focus the reality of my condition.

I am talking from an economic and visibility mountaintop that most would consider enviable. Regardless of our success, white America reminds all blacks with painful regularity that we are not viewed as equals. Whether we are rich or poor, dark skinned or light, prominent or obscure—sooner or later, we are reminded that we are not wanted.

So I say, let's study the sallow superman. Let's find out why he wants to oppress my people. I hold no quarter with those who cannot accept me as a human equal.

One final comment about race. I am convinced that greed is at the base of the problem. The racist and the materialist are the same person.

The poison of racism is poured into society's mainstream by the "haves." They already have too much wealth. Through their control of the mass media as owners and advertisers, they have conditioned masses of poor whites into thinking that the pitifully small progress the black race makes is a threat to whites.

180

So I now go through each day, as countless blacks do, dealing with a white race that is difficult to trust. Even good jobs are not enough. For whites who have trouble with my attitudes, let me cite the following explanation. The quality in our personality that makes us love the nonviolent teachings of Doctor King at the same time makes us embrace the call to self-defense of Malcolm X.

The next time you see me on your TV screen or in person, do not be fooled by my calm exterior. If I smile, it does not mean that I am not also angry. White America has created the environment of hate and hurt, so please don't ask me to be nice and banish this trait in my personality. When men, women, and children of all races are treated not "equal," but genuinely the *same*, then and only then will I reconsider my stance.

I invite blacks who are upwardly mobile, or who have already "made it," to join with me in my anger and concern. I ask that you not separate yourselves from the masses of our race and our common predicament. Never forget that the benefits you enjoy were made possible by the struggles of the masses.

I admire any group of people who have caught hell and made up their minds that it won't happen again. I respect any people who unite against oppression. Blacks should adopt that attitude, and we should become involved in some collective way to improve our common condition. I would not presume to prescribe what they should do—only that they do *something*.

I can't go along with so many members of my race who spend large amounts of money to keep the clothing industry, the disco industry, the automobile industry, and the cosmetics industry prosperous. Some consumer dollars should be diverted to an investment in black-owned and -operated enterprises. We have the capacity within our own race to solve many of our own problems.

There is no reason why we should allow an organization like the National Association for the Advancement of Colored People

181

to fall into financial difficulties, while we keep America's recording industry flourishing. The amount of money spent on record albums and tapes is enough to finance several new black colleges.

My brothers and sisters who care nothing about race and everything about profits could join us, if only out of self-interest. If we invest in building up the economic resources of our people, lawyers and doctors would have more black clients able to pay higher fees, and elected officials would have more clout in the legislative halls.

The money that black fraternal organizations spend on conventions, parades, group travel to foreign countries, parties, clothes, publications, and dances could be put to better use. The collective potential power that lies within our churches could really make a difference. If all the black churches in America pooled a portion of their funds toward a common cause that cut across sectarian lines, we could put a scare into the hearts of those who laugh at us today.

Blacks are a badly fragmented people, seemingly not able to rally behind causes of significance. We have been taught to distrust anything black. We would rather patronize a white-owned business than one of our own. We are unwilling to go out of our way to support a black enterprise in our own communities. Black people in New York alone spend tremendous amounts of money in white-owned hotels for dances, conventions, and expos. Add to that what is spent in Atlanta, Washington, D.C., Los Angeles, and Chicago, and we're talking big dollars. Money may not be power, but it can *buy* power.

Black institutions are dying because we let them die. Communities are decaying because we spend our money outside our turf. The sad truth is that whites are more active in investing in the black community than blacks are. There is no reason why whites should control the real estate and business in black communities. The reverse wouldn't be tolerated. Let's invest in and patronize our own, and where we don't have the organizations to supply a demand, let's create them.

Black adults must regain and retain the heritage of values of our ancient and noble race. It is something that we seem to have lost during our journey from native Africa to this land. We must have a more solid credo to live by than a quest for dollars, and a stronger moral anchor to hold our lives steady. We must develop a sense of principle and commitment and then pass these values on to our young.

Adults must let children know that there are certain modes of behavior that we will not condone. We must compel them to be more courteous. We must insist that they be more studious. We must recite to them the story of our struggles as a people and give them a sense of history and thus a sense of purpose.

I do not believe in being permissive with young people. In my studies of African cultures, I found that the young people are strictly disciplined. Thus the elders never worry about backtalk or violence from their children.

We must stop and rethink what we are and are not doing with our children. Kids appreciate loving discipline, even though they will rarely admit it. Looking back on my own upbringing, I remember many days that I felt under the thumb of the most unjust and tyrannical parents who ever lived. I thank them today for keeping me in line. I only wish they had been more severe. I would have been a better person for it.

My parents were uncompromising on the issue of good manners. There was no possibility of discussion or negotiation with them on this. Using profanity or being loud in the presence of elders was unthinkable. I knew that such behavior meant certain pain from the razor strop. We cannot permit our children to run unbridled through their youth, because the habits formed in youth determine the manner in which they will live their adult

183

life. We should teach our young that they have a responsibility to rebel against social injustice, while never failing to honor the traditions of respect for family, community, and race.

We may best impress this lesson on our children by acting out what we try to teach them. Many young people are confused and disoriented because they see no consistent behavior pattern in the lives of the adults around them. We should be more involved in our communities and perhaps revive a commitment in the church and political involvement. We should talk more and watch television less. Discussions should be shared with the children.

These things must be initiated early in the life of a child, because once they reach the teenage years, they are more heavily influenced by their peers and the outside environment. I have five children of my own, and I want the highest standards of thought and behavior for them. Whether they become bricklayers or businesspersons, I care most about their moral fabric. I want them to be certain about the basics of reason, manners, discretion, decorum, and taste.

I have many shortcomings as a parent. I have been away from home too much. I should have communicated with my children more and spent more time with them. I regret my shortcomings deeply, and I therefore hope that my children will forgive me for them and remember the concerns and values that I have given them in our few precious moments together.

I pray that they will recall these worthy values, not because they are my own, but because they belonged to my parents. I want my children to wear the same beautiful and strong moral garment. We must harken back to the values of our past formative years and make certain that we instill them in our offspring.

America's youth is in a quandary today. More than seventy-five percent of the high school and college students in the New York metropolitan area are into some kind of "getting high" activity. Our young, who were once our pride and joy, have become a source of terror. We parents have abdicated responsibility (for many reasons) and have not given our children the attention, love, and discipline they so badly require.

We no longer have family gatherings because the television tube gobbles up the hours at home. We have permitted our children to be fed a steady diet of mediocre trash and have allowed them to believe that the most significant achievement possible is in making money and possessing material things. Adults must chart other goals for their children and teach them the lessons of goodness.

Our young men and women must see that they have a responsibility to continue the fight against racism and oppression. No matter how fat the wallet, they can never gain the respect of the world as long as so many others of their race are catching it. Moreover, if we don't watch out for each other, we will sooner or later all go under.

I am upset about the low reading scores of black youth. I have interviewed college graduates who could barely read or write; yet reading and writing are essential skills for navigating in today's world. The keys to solving our problems as a people are found in research. Youths should use time for reading philosophy, sociology, history, essays, and poetry.

Those who destroyed the civil rights movement of the 1950s and 1960s did so by means of extensive study and analysis of the many groups and people at the forefront of our struggle. We can overcome only through similar intensive study and analysis. Our young should become sophisticated about community, national, and international politics.

Black youths should consider the great debt they owe to those who struggled and fought yesterday for their freedom today. Remember that black youth was in the vanguard of that struggle. Examine carefully the young freedom fighters of yesterday. Look at the sacrifices they made—how they deferred "getting ahead" in order to fight racism. Many left school to engage in this serious battle, and some were permanently injured, while others gave their lives. They sacrificed and suffered because of a strong set of convictions and principles.

I ask my young brothers and sisters today to compare their current profiles with those of their forerunners. If you met them today, could you justify what you are about? What would they say about your·values? Would those who fought and died to make today better for you approve of what you are into?

There is strong evidence that the youth movement of yesterday was extinguished by those powerful few in this nation who were threatened by it. If today's youth bear little resemblance to yesterday's youth, it may be because of the many narcotic devices that render them inoperable.

I strongly emphasize to youth my feelings about drugs, liquor, pills, and other means of getting high. I say, stay sober; you will never be able to solve your problems if you are high. Those who oppress us relax when they see we are spaced out. You pose a far greater threat to your enemies when sober. If you were going into the ring against Muhammad Ali, and in passing his dressing room, you saw him puffing on a·reefer, you'd probably feel confident of having a chance against him in the ring. You would know that his reflexes would be off and that his equilibrium and timing would be bad. On the other hand, you probably wouldn't get into the ring with him at all if he was sober and fit. I wouldn't!

If young brothers and sisters of today agree that black people are in serious trouble, we may be able to agree that it will take clear thinking to improve the situation. Clear thinking is impossible while high. Black youths spend a fortune daily purchasing substances that will "blow their minds." Many adults seek such escape also. We are damaging our brains and lowering our effectiveness, while making others rich in doing so.

I am convinced that TV is at least partly responsible for much of the negativism that today's youth is engaged in. I am also convinced that TV can redirect the behavior patterns of today's youth into positive channels. But the TV industry has to *really* want to do this before it can happen.

In bringing to a close this very personal account, I would like to make a parting statement to the television industry. Thank you for teaching me so much. I deeply appreciate the professional and technical expertise you have given me. I also appreciate certain of the relationships I have developed with those in the business.

I respect some of my colleagues, while others I have no respect for whatsoever. I have been a long-time critic and irritant to the television industry, and I feel that role is my responsibility, at least until broadcast quality and standards improve.

Many in this business say I am too serious. I believe I am not serious enough. The condition of black people today is serious to me, and that condition requires serious action.

I will be preoccupied with the question of race until racism is dead.

AUTHOR'S NOTE

After I completed the text of this book, and while the type was being set, certain events occurred that influence or bear upon some of the areas I wrote about. For this reason—and much to the consternation of the publisher, who wants to get on with the printing—I have decided to make these additional comments.

In Jamaica, the picture has changed considerably. In elections in late October 1980, Prime Minister Michael Manley was decisively defeated by the conservative Edward Seaga. It would not be fair to attempt to appraise the Seaga administration this early. However, Manley still stands tall in my estimation, and I feel that his defeat represents a loss not only to Jamaica, but to the poor throughout the hemisphere.

As I have stated, Manley was one of the loudest and clearest voices crying out for a new order of things in Jamaica and throughout the world. He was tireless in his efforts to provide a better life for the poor. His defeat is symbolic of the move to the political right that is taking place in this hemisphere, a move that bodes ill for the oppressed.

In this regard, it is interesting—and frightening—to note that during the Manley administration, other countries and international financial organizations refused to lend money to Jamaica. Yet as this is written, in December 1980, the International

Monetary Fund has promised to negotiate a multilevel loan of hundreds of millions of dollars to the Jamaican government under Seaga. This agreement will involve the World Bank as well. Conditions in Jamaica will undoubtedly improve, but I suspect that the benefits will accrue primarily to foreign interests and the upper class. I also suspect that in time, the people of Jamaica will come to recognize the validity of Manley's struggle.

One last note: Because of my criticisms of the TV industry, readers may presume that I have no respect for any white individuals, especially within the industry. This is not so. My criticisms still stand; nevertheless, I continue to work in TV. This would not be possible unless some executive saw validity in my contributions. It is only fair that I make this point.